COOKIN' UP GOOD HEALTH

Somethin'
To Shout
About!

Donna Green-Goodman, MPH

COOKIN' UP GOOD HEALTH!
Recipe Collection

Donna Green-Goodman, MPH

Cover Design
Still Shoutin'
A Health Education Consulting Firm
Clipart-Microsoft Suite
Photos
E IV Photography

Layout – Still Shoutin', E IV

ISBN 978-0-9675640-2-9
Copyright 2008
Donna Green-Goodman, MPH

Published by: Still Shoutin'
P.O. Box 3306
Huntsville, Alabama 35811
www.stillshoutin.com

Printed by: Remnant Publications
649 East Chicago Road
Coldwater, Michigan 49036
www.remnantpublications.com

This collection of recipes is written in memory of my family.

MOMMY
Shirley Ann Bishop Green
July 31, 1936 – January 29, 2006
For teaching me the basics and giving me a love of cooking!!

DADDY
Donald Joseph Green
December 10, 1935 – August 10, 1997
For teaching me how to follow my heart and create tasty dishes!!

BROTHER
Stephen Jeffrey Green
October 28, 1961 – August 24, 2001
For ALWAYS being willing to taste my dishes and honestly evaluate them!!

I miss you all sooooo much and am looking forward to being reunited with you and joining you at the welcome table!!

Donald, Shirley and Stephen Green
Donna and Eddie Goodman
At our nieces wedding.
We had a blast!!

ACKNOWLEDGEMENTS

The Cookin' Up Good Health Recipe Collection would have never happened if I had not been blessed to interact with and teach so many people who were interested in improving their lifestyles. Since 1996, I have been privileged to conduct lifestyle seminars, cooking classes and very recently teach Vegetarian Cuisine classes at Oakwood University. While many I have met were excited about the recipes I introduced them to from my first book Somethin' to Shout About!!, so many more wanted me to convert some of their favorite foods for them. And so, what you have here is my answer to that challenge, foods that are familiar, but now have healthier ingredients without sacrificing flavor. And, of course, if you want to be sure you get them right, you must get a copy of the Cookin' Up Good Health DVD series as well. It has been quite a journey but truly a labor of love. A very special thanks to all of you who have touched my life and helped to make this dream come true!!

The Creator God – who giveth gifts liberally

Edward T. Goodman, III, my love, life partner
and the wind beneath my wings

Edward T. Goodman, IV, my son and my inspiration

Ruth Faye Davis, Ph. D.

Office of Minority Health, State of Georgia
PRAISE 97.5 FM
The late Connie Flint
Rhodell Lewis

Health Ministries of the following churches
Cascade United Methodist Church
Ben Hill United Methodist Church
New Birth Missionary Baptist Church
Greater Piney Grove Baptist Church
Decatur Seventh-day Adventist Church
Light of the World Church
Powerhouse Temple of Deliverance
Oakwood University Church of Seventh-day Adventists

Midtown Urology – James Bennett, MD
Morehouse School of Medicine – National Center for Primary
Care
Oakhurst Medical Center – William Murrain

Babies Etc., - Jacqueline Sylvester, MD

Attendees at the
Lifestyle for Better Health Seminars
Cookin' Up Good Health Cooking Schools

My Remarkable Students at Oakwood University
Jes'Us Productions

Rwanda, Aunt June, Aunt Barbara, Nancy, Stephanie, Dr.
Scott Grivas, Aunt Bertha, Aunt Blanche, Audrey

COOKIN' UP GOOD HEALTH RECIPE COLLECTION

Cookin' Up Good Health Classes

Still Shoutin!!!

My professional career has been dedicated to teaching others how to improve their health. From 1994-1995, I worked for an NBLIC cancer prevention project at Morehouse School of Medicine in Atlanta, GA. The many years I had already spent doing community health education had quite convinced me of the connection between lifestyle choices and disease and I practiced what I preached. In 1995, I joined the Office of Nutrition for the state of Georgia as a Health Promotion Specialist and began the fun task of teaching our employees and the state we served how to make exercise and good dietary choices a part of their lives as they sought to improve their health. I was having the time of my life! So, you can imagine my shock and dismay when in 1996 I was diagnosed with invasive, aggressive, metastatic breast cancer, with spread to 6 of 17 lymph nodes. My prognosis, which included a recommendation for chemotherapy, stem-cell transplant, more chemotherapy, radiation and tamoxifen, was that even with all that treatment, I only had about 2-5 years to live, tops! I was devastated.

So, I really began to do my own research into lifestyle and disease and was absolutely convinced of its value and especially the benefits of plants foods. Nowhere in the literature could I find substantiated data that said that plant foods were linked to the development of chronic disease! As a matter of fact, I found quite the opposite. National cancer organizations, heart disease studies, diabetes educators and the American Dietetic Association were all documenting the amazing and recently discovered benefits of plant foods. I was convinced.

I decided to embrace a diet that was totally plant-based! My family and a number of friends joined me as well. I chose a physician that believed in the benefits of healthy lifestyle choices in the prevention and reversal of chronic disease. I included only radiation in my "traditional" treatment plan for the breast cancer. And, I had a lot of loooooong conversations with God. Faith in the Creator had always been the foundation of my life. Now, however, it took on a whole new meaning. I discovered that the BEST WAY to health did indeed include the principles that were found in the classic Breslow and Belloc study. Get plenty of regular rest, exercise daily and outside in the sunlight and fresh air, eat a diet that is based on plant foods, avoid harmful foods/substances, drink plenty of water and develop strong and meaningful spiritual relationships-which to me is the power of the Divine.

And, that my friends, is when the script changed. Six months after my diagnosis, my health had so improved that I was convinced that this was the only way to live. Talk about shoutin'! That's when the shoutin' started! I determined to tell as many people as I could that they could indeed reverse their chronic diseases and recapture their health if they were willing to make some decisions and follow through on them.

It's been more than twelve years now. I am so thankful and I am still shoutin'! I shout, not just for how my life has been impacted, but for how I have seen others' lives changed for the better. I shout for the people who are being convinced that they can take control of their lifestyles and save their own lives and health. I shout with:

My son Ivey, who after 7 years was allergy free!!

Aunt Barbara who after some convincing was able to improve her diabetes readings and get off her insulin;

My husband's patient who couldn't wait to put on her church shoes again and go to Sunday service and get her praise on;

My husband's other patient who cancelled his foot amputation after lifestyle and rehab intervention that restored circulation;

Pastors William Flippen and M.J. Pace who improved their own health and then challenged their congregations to join them and receive God's greatest gift;

A member of Cascade United Methodist church who had been trying to conceive for a while and was finally able to have that baby after she changed her lifestyle;

My friend Virginia Lucear who was on a mission to "save her breasts" after being diagnosed with breast cancer and not just survives but thrives!

A recent attendee at one of my cooking schools who watched a breast lump shrink after she changed her lifestyle;

Former Morehouse School of Medicine president, James Gavin, III, who loved the banana pudding when he tasted it at a health conference.

James Bennett, MD who really reached out to African-American men in metro-Atlanta and challenged them to take control of their health....like he does.....!!!

With my friend Jacqueline Sylvester, MD who would not rest until I completed this collection so that she could share it with her patients;

The people who decided that they wanted to lose weight and keep it off;

Those people who decided that collard greens and cornbread do not have to have fatback or turkey wings to taste good!!

My students, who are convinced and are making it their business to convince their parents and other loved ones who are suffering unnecessarily from chronic diseases;

For the men who experienced side effects of hypertension medications and/or atherosclerosis and were able to reverse it and get their lovin' back on;

For the many who have been able to discard, with physician approval, their medications!!!!!

And, I shout for you!! Whatever your health condition, no one can make as big a difference in your health as you can! YOU and you alone live with you every day. When you decide (will) yourself to make a change and follow through on it........you will be shoutin' too!!

If you are ready to make some serious dietary changes as part of your lifestyle improvement plan, you will enjoy this collection. I recommend these recipes especially for those who are beginning to make changes and need somewhere to start. Follow the recipes as written, they have been taste-tested by regular folk and I listened to what they said. Then, if you need to, make your own adjustments. If you are already along on the journey and prefer not to eat soy, gluten, natural sugars or wheat, feel free to adjust the recipe to suit your tastes. If your family or loved ones are coming along slowly, cook it up and serve it without an introduction and watch what happens!!!!!!!!! Include your kids in the process. My cousins Leslie and June and I still remember learning how to make jelly and yeast rolls and mac 'n cheese and apple pie with my mom when we were kids!! It's a memory that we cherish dearly and speak of often. Then share your joy of success with others you may know!

And, remember, lifestyle is still the most under-prescribed medical treatment for chronic disease. Yet, when prescribed and faithfully applied, it is the most powerful medical treatment available and has no negative side effects. Lifestyle really is your BEST WAY to health! And, that is somethin' to shout about!!

Get busy changing your lifestyle!! And you will be shoutin' too!!

Blessed is she that believed for there shall be a performance of those things which were told her from the Lord. Luke 1:45

MAKING THE SWITCH

As I conduct cooking classes, I am discovering over and over again, that people will change if the recommended new foods don't sacrifice on taste. Here are some ideas to help in preserving taste for your switch to a new lifestyle, or to use in preparing foods for your vegetarian friends.

Arrowroot: White powdery substance used for thickening. I sometimes use in place of cornstarch

BAKON: A smoked yeast with a natural hickory smoke flavor. I use it in all my beans, and in seasoning vegetables. Wonderful no-fat, no-cholesterol option. Available at ABC (Adventist Book Center) stores.

Bragg's Liquid Aminoes: An unfermented soy sauce substitute. Made from soybeans, high in amino acids and other minerals, and lower in sodium than soy sauce.

Carob: A wonderful substitute for chocolate, this comes from the nutritious locust bean pod. It is naturally sweet, high in vitamin A, calcium, phosphorus, potassium, iron and magnesium. Has no caffeine and much less fat. It is available in a powdered form. You can also buy it processed into carob chips. Choose the malt sweetened ones and use as you would chocolate chips.

Cashews: Classed with nuts, cashews are actually a tropical fruit. They are lower in fat than most nuts and yield a creamy sauce when blended with water, and thicken when heated. You can find them raw, roasted or as butter. When using them in a recipe for sauce, etc., use the raw ones, but wash them first as they tend to be dirty. My friend Jennifer and I sometimes substitute almonds in equal amounts when we don't have cashews on hand.

Coriander: Is the fruit of the coriander herb. Recommended as a cinnamon substitute, as cinnamon can be irritating to the digestive tract.

Ener-G Egg Replacer: Non-dairy, powdered binding agent. It can be used as a substitute for eggs in baked goods. Follow directions on box when using it.

Featherweight Baking Powder: A baking powder that does not contain harmful aluminum or baking soda, which is a digestive tract irritant and can kill certain vitamins.

Flavorings: Non-alcoholic flavorings are best. The Spicery Shoppe and Frontier are two brands that I recommend and use.

Florida Crystals: Trade name for evaporated cane juice. This sugar product has not been processed as much as white sugar. I recommend its use occasionally.

Herbs: Fresh or dried, when I realized the marvelous benefits of herbs, beyond flavoring, I planted an herb garden on my deck. Imagine cutting exactly your favorite herb in the amount you need for a dish you are preparing. I grew parsley, sage, rosemary, thyme, apple mint, basil and oregano. They were all so easy to do.

Lemon Juice: A necessary replacement for harmful vinegar, which is fermented and contains acetic acid. I buy fresh lemons, squeeze them, refrigerate the juice and use in any recipe that calls for vinegar. Limonoids, are a potent phytochemical found in citrus fruits.

McKay's Chicken Style or Beef Style Seasoning: My friend Debbie calls Chicken-Style the "Wonder" seasoning. She uses it on everything except fruit. Both seasonings are vegetarian and add a meaty flavor without the meat. The "No MSG" type is recommended. Available at ABC (Adventist Book Center) stores. Health food stores would probably order it.

Nutritional Yeast Flakes: This is an edible brewer's yeast. It comes "flaked", is yellow in color, and is the secret to making "cheez" sauces. It is high in B vitamins. Red Star is the brand I use.

PA's Pickles: These pickles are made with lemon juice instead of vinegar. They come sliced, in strips and as relish. Available at ABC (Adventist Book Center) stores.

Pimento: A heart shaped member of the pepper family. It has a sweet, mild flavor and can be added to dishes for color and/or flavor. Look for it in your grocery store on the aisle with condiments. I grew some this summer in my herb garden.

Roma: A coffee substitute made from grains. Available at ABC stores and most health food stores.

Soy Parmesan Cheese: Alternative to dairy Parmesan cheese. Three brands I am familiar with are Soya-Kass,

SoyCo and Soymage. Soymage is the only one of the three that does not contain the milk protein casein.

Spectrum Spread: - A non-hydrogenated spread made from vegetable oil.

Stevia: An herbal sweetener that is much sweeter than processed white sugar.

Sucanat: A granulated sugar made from organic sugar cane juice. Because it is unrefined, it still contains its original vitamins and minerals. I use it in place of brown sugar.

Turmeric: A mustard-like herb that is non-irritating to the digestive tract. It adds a wonderful color and flavor to foods. It is also being touted as having anti-cancer properties. Be careful when you start using it, it can be overpowering.

Wright's Hickory Smoke: A bottled liquid hickory smoke flavoring, that I use in barbecue sauces. This brand has no questionable ingredients.

SUGGESTED SUBSTITIONS

FOR:	USE INSTEAD
Milk	Soy Milks Rice Milks Cashew Milks Almond Milk
Buttermilk	Add 1 T. Lemon Juice to 1 cup non-dairy milk
Cheese	Commercial soy, rice Cheeses Make cashew cheese
Eggs, scrambled	Scrambled tofu
Eggs, as binder	Ener-G Egg Replacer Oats, bread crumbs, Gluten flour, flax seed gel
Chocolate	Carob
Cinnamon	Coriander
Coffee	Roma, Pero
Tea	Caffeine-free herb tea
Sugar	Fruit, fruit juice, sucanat, honey, evaporated cane juice, molasses

Black Pepper	Herbs
	Pepper Like Seasoning by
	Vegetarian Express
Hot peppers	Garlic
Beef/Chicken Flavors	McKay's Chicken or Beef Style Seasoning
Turkey Wings	BAKON Seasoning
Cracklin/Bacon	Imitqtion baco bits
Vinegar	Fresh Lemon or Lime juice
Soy Sauce	Bragg's Liquid Aminoes
Gelatin	Emes Vegetable Gelatin
Pork n' Beans	Bush's Vegetarian Baked Beans
White Rice	Brown Rice, long-grain, Short grain, instant, wild rice
White Pasta	Whole Wheat pasta
	Whole Grain Pasta
	Soy Pasta
Fatback/Lard	Olive Oil
	Earth Balance Buttery Sticks
	Earth Balance Natural Shortening

BETTER
BREAKFASTS

Simple Scrambled Tofu

Olive oil

$\frac{1}{2}$ small-medium onion

1 pound water packed tofu (drained and sliced or crumbled as desired)

$\frac{1}{4}$ - $\frac{1}{2}$ teaspoon or more turmeric

1-2 tablespoons McKay's Chicken Style, or more to taste

1-2 tablespoons Nutritional Yeast Flakes, or more to taste

In a small frying pan, sauté onion in a small amount of olive oil. Add tofu and turmeric till desired color is reached. Add McKay's Chicken Style and nutritional yeast flakes, adjusting to taste. Reduce heat, cover and simmer till seasoned through.

Serves 2-4

Breakfast Hash

This is one I came upon purely by accident. I was visiting some friends and there was not enough tofu to feed the group waiting. Through necessity, the cook invented this delicious breakfast hash. It was a really big hit at our cooking class. I sometimes make a single serving for myself. You will need equal amounts of the following ingredients:

Your favorite recipe scrambled tofu with red and green peppers-leftover works quite well
Crumbled onion flavored tater tots
Broccoli flowerets
Crumbled Vegetarian Breakfast Sausage

Into a large skillet pour a little olive oil. Brown crumbled veggie sausage until crisp. Add tater tots and keep stirring until desired color/crispness. Add broccoli flowerets, cover and let steam for about 5 minutes on low heat. Uncover and add scrambled tofu stirring in gently. Heat until tofu is warm. Serve with biscuits or whole grain toast and jelly. Serves as many or few as you'd like depending on how much you make.
(Sometimes I add one diced, raw sweet potato with the tater tots.)

Pancakes or Belgian Waffles

In a blender blend
2 cups warm water
$\frac{1}{2}$ cup raw cashews
1 cup oats
1 teaspoon salt
1/3 cup sweetener (I like honey)

In a small bowl dissolve:
$\frac{1}{2}$ teaspoon yeast in $\frac{1}{4}$ cup water

In a large bowl pour:
Blended mixture
Yeast mixture
1 $\frac{1}{2}$ cup unbleached flour
$\frac{1}{2}$ cup whole wheat flour
$\frac{1}{4}$ cup oil
1 $\frac{1}{2}$ tablespoon alcohol-free vanilla
$\frac{1}{2}$ teaspoon Featherweight baking powder

Mix. Thin with your favorite non-dairy milk to desired consistency. Mix and pour onto vegetable sprayed griddle or waffle iron.

YIELD: 4-5 Large waffles

Eddie's Pancakes

1 tablespoon EnerG egg replacer
½ cup all purpose flour
½ cup whole wheat flour (pastry or white whole wheat)
¾ - 1 cup milk (soy, rice or nut)
2 tablespoons canola oil
1 tablespoon turbinado sugar
3 teaspoons Featherweight Baking Powder
½ teaspoon salt

Measure all dry ingredients into a mixing bowl. Add milk and oil and stir until well blended. Oil a heating griddle and pour batter onto griddle. Cook pancakes until puffed and dry around edges. Turn and cook other side until golden brown. *Serve with REAL maple syrup, fruit, nuts or the following fruit sauce.*

Yield: 6-10 pancakes

Fruit Sauce

4 cups fresh or frozen strawberries or other favorite fruit (blueberries, peaches)
1-12 ounce can frozen white grape raspberry juice concentrate (white grape peach if using peaches)
1 heaping tablespoon cornstarch

Serves 6-8

Coffee Cake

1 cup whole wheat pastry flour
1 cup all-purpose, unbleached flour
¾ cup your favorite natural sugar
3 heaping teaspoons Featherweight baking powder
1 teaspoon salt
1/3 cup canola oil
1 cup vanilla soy milk, more if needed
1 tablespoon EnerG egg Replacer

Streusel-½ cup chopped nuts, 1/3 cup natural sugar, ¼ cup all-purpose unbleached flour, ½ teaspoon coriander, 3 tablespoons firm soy margarine. Mix all ingredients until crumbly.

Prepare streusel. Beat all other ingredients in a large bowl until smooth. Add a little more milk if mixture is too thick. Spread half of the batter in a rectangular or square baking dish that has been sprayed with vegetable spray. Sprinkle with half the streusel. Top with remaining batter and sprinkle with remaining streusel. Bake for about 35-40 minutes until golden brown at 350^0. Great for morning breakfast during the holidays.

Serves 6-8

Angel Biscuits

1 package active dry yeast
¼ cup warm water
1 ¼ cups WHITE whole wheat flour
1 ¼ cups unbleached flour
1 teaspoon Featherweight baking powder
1 teaspoon salt
2 tablespoons natural sugar
½ cup Earth Balance margarine
1 cup buttermilk (mix 1 cup of your favorite soy, nut or rice milk with 1 tablespoon lemon juice added)

Dissolve yeast in warm water. Sift dry ingredients into a bowl. Cut in margarine till flour is crumbly in appearance. Stir in buttermilk and yeast mixture. Mix well and refrigerate for later use OR roll dough out and cut into biscuits. Place on baking sheet, cover and let rise until nearly double – about 45 minutes. Bake in 400° oven till golden. Brush tops with melted margarine or oil.

Yield: 1 dozen

Serve with confetti cream gravy or stuff with vege sausage patties or vege ham for breakfast buffet.

Confetti Creamed "Meat" Gravy

1 cup raw cashews
2 cup water
$\frac{1}{2}$ small onion, chopped
$\frac{1}{2}$ cup sweet bell pepper (combination of red, yellow, green, orange)
$\frac{1}{2}$ cup sliced mushroom-OPTIONAL
$\frac{1}{2}$ cup your favorite veggie meat (sausage, chicken, beef, ham, bacon or diced tofu)
Favorite seasonings - NO MSG Mckay's Chicken Style seasoning, garlic powder, basil

Blend cashews in blender in 1 cup of water until smooth. Add the remaining water and blend again. Place in pot on stove on medium heat. Add vegetables and your choice veggie meat. Season with favorite seasonings to taste. Cook until thickened, stirring often. Pour into large soup bowl and serve over hot biscuits.

Yield: About 3-4 cups gravy

Grits

6 cups water

2 cups Logan Turnpike Mill Whole Grain Grits (white or yellow)

1 ½ -2 teaspoons salt (optional, as desired)

Place grits in saucepan. Add water and optional salt. Place on medium heat, cover and let simmer to desired consistency. Serve with your choice of veggie ham bits, soy cheese, veggie fish, better biscuits and fried green tomatoes.

Because these grits are not refined, (they contain all the nutrients found in the grain of corn), they cook up creamier and do not get hard when leftover. They're the only grits we will eat now. Check out this website for availability in your area www.loganturnpikemill.com.

Blackberry Spread

4 cups blackberries
1 teaspoon lemon juice
$\frac{1}{4}$ cup water
$\frac{1}{2}$ cup + 2 tablespoons honey
6 tablespoons cornstarch

Blend cornstarch, water, lemon juice with a handful of berries. Pour into a saucepan and add honey. Bring to a boil, stirring constantly. Add rest of berries and return to a boil, stirring constantly to prevent scorching. Chill and serve!

YIELD: About 5 cups

Apricot Marmalade

1 cup water, pineapple or apple juice
1 teaspoon lemon juice
1 cup dried apricot pieces
1 cup pitted dates

Mix ingredients in a saucepan and simmer abut ten minutes until soft. Cool, then blend together in blender until as smooth as desired. You may need to add a little more water or juice.

Yield: 1 $\frac{1}{2}$ cups

Sensational Smoothie
½ medium mango, diced
2 strips fresh pineapple
1 small peach, diced
4-6 large strawberries
Your favorite soy, nut or rice milk OR fruit juice
Alcohol-free coconut flavoring, to taste
Honey to taste (optional)

Place fruit in a blender. Add enough milk or juice to blend to desired consistency. Add coconut flavoring and optional honey to taste. ENJOY!!

VARIATION: Individually freeze the fruit in quart freezer bags. Have frozen fruit available for smoothies throughout the winter season. Frozen fruit always makes thicker smoothies.

My girlfriend Jackie freezes hers in popsicle trays for her school-aged children.

Yield: about 3 cups

Blueberry Muffins

1 cup whole wheat flour (pastry or white whole wheat)
1 cup unbleached all purpose flour
1 tablespoon Featherweight Baking Powder, heaping
1 teaspoon salt
1 tablespoon EnerG egg replacer
1 cup vanilla soy milk
1/3 cup canola oil
1 cup fresh or frozen blueberries (thawed)

OPTIONAL TOPPING

$\frac{1}{2}$ cup Earth Balance Margarine, melted OR $\frac{1}{4}$ cup canola oil
$\frac{1}{2}$ cup evaporated cane juice sugar

Preheat oven to 400°. Spray muffin pan. Mix dry ingredients in a mixing bowl. In a separate bowl, mix liquid ingredients. Pour liquid mixture and blueberries into dry mixture and mix. Batter will be lumpy. Spoon batter into muffin pan. Bake 20-22 minutes or until golden brown. Immediately remove muffins from pan and dip tops of muffins in optional melted margarine then in sugar. Serve warm.

Yield: 1 dozen

Sweet Rolls
Dough
1 package yeast
$\frac{1}{2}$ cup warm water
$\frac{1}{2}$ cup warm soy, rice or nut milk
1/3 cup natural sugar
1/3 cup Earth Balance Margarine
1 teaspoon salt
2 tablespoons EnerG Egg Replacer dissolved in
2 cups white whole wheat flour AND
2 cups unbleached flour OR
4 cups whole wheat pastry flour

Pour warm water into a large bowl. Add yeast and stir till dissolved. Add milk, sugar, margarine salt and egg replacer. Stir. Add two cups of the flour and stir. Add enough of the remaining flour to make a soft dough.

Put dough on floured area and knead for about 7 minutes. Place in a bowl that has been oil-sprayed. Cover and let rise about an hour or until double in size. Punch dough down and cut in half. Roll first half into an oblong shape. Put $\frac{1}{2}$ of filling on dough. Roll, cut into 1 inch pieces and place on vegetable sprayed baking dish. Repeat process with second piece of dough. Cover and let rise until double. Bake at 375° until done, about 25-30 minutes. Let cool then cover with your favorite glaze and nuts.

Filling

2 cups unbleached flour
2 cups sucanat
2 tablespoons coriander
2 teaspoons salt
1 cup oil

Mix above ingredients in a bowl. Sprinkle and spread filling onto prepared sweet roll dough.

Makes about 2 dozen

Summer Fruit Salad

1 cup each diced cantaloupe, watermelon, honeydew,
1 cup your favorite color grapes
1 cup strawberries, sliced in half
½ cup your choice orange juice or pineapple juice
½ cup chopped your favorite nut (I prefer slivered almonds)

Place prepared fruit in a bowl. Pour juice over fruit and stir. Chill. Just before serving toss in nuts. Serve.

Serves 6-8

Fruit Compote

1 cup fresh strawberries
1 cup fresh pineapple chunks
1 cup honeydew melon cubes
2 peeled, sliced bananas
1 cup fresh orange juice

Wash and dice strawberries, pineapple and honeydew melon. Peel bananas and slice. Mix the above ingredients in a bowl and add the freshly squeezed orange juice. Serve.

Serves 6-8

Fruit Crisp

4 cups sliced fruit (I like peaches)
1-12 ounce can fruit juice concentrate minus 1 tablespoon
1 tablespoon cornstarch
Dash salt
Vanilla
Coriander

2 cups rolled oats
1 cup whole wheat pastry flour
3 tablespoons honey
4 tablespoons canola oil
1 tablespoon fruit juice concentrate that you reserved
1 teaspoon vanilla
$\frac{1}{2}$ teaspoon salt
$\frac{1}{2}$ cup almonds

Mix first 6 ingredients and place in oven-proof dish.
Mix rest of ingredients and place over fruit. Cover with foil
and bake about 30 minutes in 350° oven. Uncover and bake
for an additional 5-10 minutes till lightly browned.

Serves 6-8

MAIN
DISHES

It's a fact, brown rice is better for you. Here are a bunch of ways to make it taste real good.

Plain Brown Rice

2 cups uncooked, long grain brown rice
5 cups water
$\frac{1}{2}$ teaspoon salt (optional)
Place rice, water and salt in an oven-proof dish. Stir. Cover and bake at 350° until water is completely absorbed and rice is dry. (1-1 $\frac{1}{2}$ hours usually). Serve plain or with your favorite dish or with the following variations. The cooked rice freezes well for future use.

Variations:

Use the INSTANT version of brown rice. Store brands work just as well as national brands.

Breakfast Rice – To 1-2 cups cooked brown rice add $\frac{1}{2}$ cup each sautéed onion and bell pepper, vege sausage or ham and leftover scrambled tofu.

Dirty Rice – To 1-2 cups cooked brown rice add $\frac{1}{2}$ cup each sautéed red and yellow onion, red, green, yellow, orange bell pepper, vege sausage, ham, chicken, fish. Dirty the rice with basil, parsley, Chicken Like Seasoning, and paprika to taste.

Yellow Rice – Saute small onion in a small amount of olive oil. Stir in instant brown rice, 1-2 teaspoons turmeric, 1-2 bay leaves, 1-2 teaspoons parsley. Add $3\frac{1}{4}$ cups hot water, season to taste with Chicken Like Seasoning. Bring to boil, reduce heat, cover and let simmer till done.

Yummy Sausage Rice

3 tablespoons olive oil
1 tablespoon annatto seeds
1 can diced green chiles
3 cloves garlic, minced
1-1 ½ cups your favorite veggie sausage, crumbled
2 bay leaves
1 cup diced tomato
3 cup cooked brown rice
Salt to taste

In skillet heat oil and add annatto seeds. Cook until oil turns yellow then remove seeds and discard. Add sausage and brown. Add tomato, bay leaves, chiles and garlic and stir till heated through. Stir in cooked rice and salt to taste. Remove bay leaves before serving.

Serves 6-8

Confetti Yellow Rice with Black Beans and Broccoli

Olive Oil
½ cup each chopped red and yellow onion
½ cup each chopped red, green, yellow, and orange bell pepper
½ cup Vege chicken broken into pieces
½ cup Vege sausage broken into pieces
½ cup Vege ham broken into pieces
1 cup chopped broccoli
1 can black beans, rinsed and drained
McKay's No MSG Chicken like seasoning
Garlic powder

Saute red and yellow onion, red, green, yellow, orange bell pepper, vege sausage, ham and, chicken. Add 1 can black beans, rinsed and drained, and 1 cup chopped raw broccoli. Stir until heated through. Add at least 2 cups cooked yellow rice (more if the crowd is bigger) and mix well, adjusting to taste with garlic powder and chicken like seasoning and your favorite seasonings as desired.

Serves 6-8

Rice with Black Beans, Corn and Salsa
Olive oil
$\frac{1}{2}$ roll veggie sausage
1 medium onion
$\frac{1}{2}$ large green bell pepper
1 box instant/quick brown rice
1 can black beans
$\frac{1}{2}$ - 1 cup fresh or frozen corn
$\frac{1}{2}$ cup vinegar-free salsa
Water to equal 3 cups
Cumin
Chicken Like Seasoning

Brown veggie sausage in olive oil. Add onion and bell pepper and sauté. Stir in rice, beans and corn. In a measuring cup, pour $\frac{1}{2}$ cup vinegar-free salsa and enough water to equal 3 cups. Add to pot. Season to taste with cumin and chicken-like seasoning. Bring to boil. Reduce heat to low and allow to simmer until water is absorbed and rice is tender.

Serves 6-8

*You can also use 2 cups old fashioned brown rice with four cups liquid.

Rice a Rooni
Small onion, chopped
Stalk of celery
1 ½ cup quick/instant brown rice
½ cup whole wheat spaghetti, broken into small pieces
4 cups water
Chicken like seasoning
Turmeric

Saute onion and celery in a small amount of olive oil. Add rice and spaghetti. Add water and season to taste with chicken like seasoning. Add about a ¼ teaspoon of turmeric. Bring to boil. Reduce heat. Let simmer until water is absorbed and rice and pasta are tender.

Serves 6-8

Paella

$\frac{1}{4}$ cup olive oil
2 garlic cloves, minced
1 medium onion, chopped
2 tablespoons fresh Cilantro, chopped
2 tablespoons fresh basil, chopped
1 tablespoon dried thyme
1/8 ounce saffron
1 Box Instant Brown Rice
 4 cups water
$\frac{1}{2}$ cup your favorite veggie chicken
$\frac{1}{2}$ cup your favorite veggie sausage
$\frac{1}{2}$ cup your favorite veggie fish
2 tomatoes, diced
$\frac{3}{4}$ cup frozen green peas
McKay's Chicken Style Seasoning, to taste
Salt to taste

In a large pot, sauté garlic, onions, herbs and saffron in the olive oil. Add rice and stir-fry. Add water to sautéed mixture, adding Mckay's chicken style to taste. Bring to boil and reduce heat. Let simmer until rice is done. While rice is cooking, warm veggie meats and dice tomatoes. When rice is done, fold in veggie meats, tomatoes and green peas. Adjust seasonings to taste. ENJOY!!!!!

Serves 10

Guyanan Spinach Cook-Up Rice

1 box instant brown rice
1 medium onion, chopped
1 medium red or green pepper, chopped
1 small box frozen, chopped spinach, thawed
2 cloves garlic, crushed
sprig of thyme
1 5.5 ounce can premium coconut milk PLUS enough water to
equal 4 cups
salt to taste
olive oil

In a large pot sauté the onion in a little olive oil for a few
minutes. Add the peppers, spinach and garlic. Continuing
sautéing for about 5-7 more minutes. Add thyme, coconut
milk/water mixture and salt to taste. Cover and cook on low
heat until rice is done.

*This recipe was introduced to me by my friend Stephanie. My
husband, who I one day will prove is a geechee, absolutely loved it!*

Serves 6-8

Broccoli and Rice Casserole

3 cups water
1 cup raw cashews
$\frac{1}{4}$ teaspoon paprika
2 cups instant brown rice, uncooked
2 cups veggie turkey or chicken, chopped
2 cups fresh or frozen broccoli flowerets
1 cup soy cheddar cheese
Favorite seasonings – NO MSG McKay's Chicken Style
seasoning, garlic powder

In blender, blend cashews and water until very smooth. In a
large skillet pour cashew mixture and paprika. Bring to a boil
and taste, adding your favorite seasonings. Stir in rice,
veggie meat and broccoli. Sprinkle with soy cheese. Cover.
Cook on low heat until thoroughly heated and rice is tender.

Serves 6

Aunt Betty's Louisiana Red Beans and Rice

Olive oil

1 ½ -2 cups your favorite veggie sausage, chopped or sliced

1 medium onion, chopped

1 stalk celery, chopped

1 medium green pepper chopped

2-3 cloves garlic, chopped

1 can red kidney beans

2 ½ cups brown rice, uncooked

1-2 tablespoons dried parsley

1-2 bay leaves

Juice from beans and enough water to equal 5 cups

McKay's NO MSG Chicken Style Seasoning

Pepper Like Seasoning

In a large enough pan heat small amount of olive oil. Brown vege sausage. Add onion, celery, green pepper and garlic. Stir fry for about 2 minutes. Add kidney beans, parsley bay leave and rice. Add 5 cups liquid (juice from beans plus water to make 5 cups). Season to taste with McKay's and Like Pepper. Bring to a boil, then reduce heat and let simmer till rice is done.

Serves 8-10

Supper in a Skillet
Olive oil
1 small onion, chopped
$\frac{1}{2}$ bell pepper, chopped
1-1 $\frac{1}{2}$ cups your favorite veggie burger,
1 box whole wheat pasta, (macaroni, penne pasta, or other choice)
1 28 ounce jar your favorite spaghetti sauce
Garlic powder, basil and any other favorite Italian seasonings

In a skillet, (preferably cast-iron) brown veggie burger. Add onion and bell pepper and sauté for about 5 minutes. Stir in entire bag of pasta. Add jar of spaghetti sauce and one jar full of water. Stir, adding garlic and basil and other seasonings to taste. Bring to a boil, then reduce heat, cover and let simmer till noodles are tender. (You might need to add some more water if mixture gets too thick). Adjust seasonings again and serve with broccoli/cheez sauce and garlic bread.

Variation: Add corn, tomato sauce and Mexican seasonings instead of spaghetti sauce.

Serves 6-8

Judy's Slammin' Mac 'n Cheese

2 cups heaping, soy macaroni noodles or your favorite whole grain
4 cups water
2 tablespoons soy margarine
1 tablespoon heaping, soy sour cream
1 tablespoon lemon juice
2 teaspoons salt
1 pkg. Follow Your Heart cheddar cheese, grated
$\frac{1}{2}$ pkg. Follow Your Heart mozzarella cheese, grated
$\frac{1}{2}$ pkg. Follow Your Heart Monterey Jack cheese, grated
$\frac{1}{2}$ -1 cups Nutritional yeast flakes, or more to taste
2 cups plain soy milk, more/less to your preference
     Garlic powder, Chicken like Seasoning, Turmeric, salt
     to taste

Grate cheese and mix evenly. Boil macaroni in the water to desired tenderness. Drain and immediately add margarine, $\frac{3}{4}$ of the cheese and the sour cream. Stir, letting the heat from the macaroni melt the margarine, cheese and sour cream. Add nutritional yeast flakes, lemon juice, salt, and milk. Add additional seasonings to taste. Place in a casserole dish and add remaining grated cheese to the top. Cover and bake at 350° about 30 minutes (cheese on top should be melted). Uncover and turn the oven to broil. Broil macaroni to desired brownness. Remove from oven and serve.

Serves 8-10

Like Tuna Casserole

1 regular-sized box uncooked, whole grain spaghetti
2 cups water
1 cup raw cashews
2 cups your favorite veggie tuna
1 jar (2 ½ oz) sliced mushrooms, drained OR ½ c. fresh, sliced mushrooms
1 jar (2 ½ oz.) diced pimento, drained OR ½ c. fresh, diced red bell pepper
2 cups soy cheddar cheese, grated (optional)
No MSG McKay's Chicken Style Seasoning, Garlic powder
Soy Parmesan Cheese (optional)

Cook spaghetti according to package directions. In a blender, blend cashews and water. Pour into large pot and heat until thickening is noted. Add tuno, mushrooms, pimento, veggie shreds and cooked spaghetti. Stir and add seasonings as desired. (Add a little water to thin, if necessary) Pour into a casserole dish and sprinkle with optional soy parmesan cheese. Cook covered in 350° oven until bubbly, about 30 minutes. Uncover and let cook until lightly browned.

Serves 6-8.

*It's delicious without mushrooms also! Add peas with the pimento.

Corn Casserole

1 16 oz. can cream style corn
1 cup frozen white corn
1 cup frozen yellow corn
2 cups plain or vanilla soymilk
3 tablespoons each flour and Earth Balance Margarine, melted OR canola oil
1 teaspoon sugar
½ teaspoon salt
1 tablespoon EnerG egg replacers
2 tablespoons vegetarian ham bits, optional

Mix all ingredients in a mixing bowl. Pour into an oven-proof dish. Cover and bake at 350° until done, about 45 minutes. Uncover and let brown, if you like. Remove from oven and let sit until set.

Serves 6-8

Oat Burgers

3 cups water
½ cup Bragg's Liquid Aminoes
3 cups quick oats
3 tablespoons oil
1 tablespoon honey
1 tablespoon onion powder
1 tablespoon sage
3 tablespoons yeast flakes
1 tablespoon garlic powder
1 tablespoon Italian seasoning
1 tablespoon BAKON

Combine water and seasonings in a 4-quart saucepan and bring to a boil. Add oats and cook over medium heat for 5-10 minutes. Cool slightly and shape by hand into burgers or use a burger press. Place on baking sheet that has been sprayed with vegetable oil spray. Bake at 350° for 15 minutes on each side.

Serves 6-8

My mom used to teach our lifestyle guests how to make these burgers. If you shape then by using a tablespoon, they are more like little sausages. When I shared it with my Oakwood University Students, one of them Beatrice Dolce, made her own alterations. Her variation follows on the next page!

B's Blessed Burgers

3 cups water

1/3 - ½ cup Bragg's Liquid Aminoes

3 cups quick oats

3 tablespoon oil

1 tablespoon honey

1 tablespoon onion powder

1 tablespoon basil

3 tablespoons yeast flakes

1 tablespoon garlic powder

1 tablespoon Italian seasoning

1 tablespoon McKay's Chicken Style Seasoning

1 tablespoon Oregano

½ -1 cup Pecan Meal (use as much as you desire, it's a binding ingredient)

½ package of crumbled tofu

Combine water and seasonings in a 4-quart saucepan and bring to a boil. Add tofu and cook over medium heat for 5-10 minutes. Then add oats and let it cook over medium heat for 5-10 minutes. Cool slightly and shape by hand into burgers or use a burger press. Place on baking sheet that has been sprayed with vegetable oil spray. Bake at 350° for 15 minutes on each side.

Serves 6-8

Donna's Delicious Tofu Loaf

1 pound firm, water packed tofu
3-4 cups Grape-Nuts flakes
¼ cup olive oil
1 onion, chopped
1 bell pepper, chopped
½ cup mushrooms, chopped-OPTIONAL
½ cup pecan meal, or more as desired
1 cup plain soy milk or more till desired consistency
Sage, garlic powder, McKay's NO MSG Chicken style
seasoning, Bragg's Liquid Aminoes to taste

Drain the tofu. Mash or crumble in a mixing bowl. Sauté the onion, bell pepper and mushrooms, in the olive oil. Add rest of ingredients and stir until well blended. Place in an 8x8 or loaf pan baking dish. Cover and bake covered at 325° for 45 minutes. Uncover and continue baking until it reaches the desired brownness. Slice and serve with gravy and mashed potatoes. YUM! YUM!

Serves 6-8

This is a great update on traditional "cottage cheese" loaf. Enjoy!

Auntie Debbie's Best Big Frank's

1 can Big Frank's, original, sliced (save the broth)
1 cup bell pepper, chopped, your choice of color
1 onion, medium, chopped
1 jar of your favorite spaghetti or marinara sauce
Olive oil

In a small amount of olive oil, sauté onion and bell pepper.
Add sliced Big Franks, stirring until lightly browned. Add
your choice of sauce and the broth from the Big Franks.
Cover and let simmer on low heat for about 20 minutes.
Serve over rice.

Serves 6-8

*Auntie Debbie made this for my son when he was going
through a particularly hard time. It was a hit! We now
serve it when he has his college friends over and I need
something quick, easy and tasty!*

Edna's Meat Loaf

1/3 cup olive oil
1 medium onion, chopped
1 medium bell pepper, chopped
3 cloves garlic, chopped
1 roll, Gimme Lean Sausage
$\frac{1}{2}$ bag Morningstar Farms Grillers Crumbles
$\frac{1}{2}$ - $\frac{3}{4}$ loaf whole wheat bread, cubed
$\frac{1}{2}$ package Follow Your Heart cheddar cheese, grated
Onion powder, Mckay's Chicken Style, garlic powder, liquid
smoke, Bragg's Aminoes, sage to taste
Plain soy milk

Saute onion, bell pepper, garlic in olive oil. In a large bowl mix
sautéed veggies with all other ingredients. Work with hands
until mixed well. Season to taste. If necessary, add a little
plain soy milk. Place in glass baking dish and cover. Bake at
350^0 for 30-45 minutes. Remove from oven, pour enough of
Donna's Momma's Barbecue Sauce to cover top and bake
uncovered another 15 minutes. Slice and serve.

Serves 8-10

*My girlfriend Edna introduced this to my husband and
son. DeeLish!! Often veggie meat loaves contain nuts.
This one does not and my cousin Gil, who is allergic to
nuts LOVES IT!!!!!!!! This is my version. Thanks Edna!!*

Marvelous Meatballs

1 roll Gimme Lean Sausage
$\frac{1}{2}$ roll Gimme Lean Beef
$\frac{1}{2}$ bag Morningstar Farms Grillers crumbles or other veggie burger
$\frac{1}{2}$ cup pecan meal
1 cup your favorite soy cheddar cheese, grated
1 medium onion, chopped
$\frac{1}{2}$ medium green or red bell pepper, chopped
1 tablespoon olive oil
Garlic powder, sage and other favorite seasonings to taste

Mix all ingredients in a bowl. Shape into pecan-sized balls. Fry in small amount of oil, or bake in oven. Pour Donna's Mommas' Barbecue Sauce over meatballs, cover and bake in oven at 350^0 till bubbly.

Variation: Add Italian seasonings, fry or bake, and add to spaghetti sauce. Serve over spaghetti!

Makes about 3 dozen small meatballs

Donna's Momma's Barbeque Sauce

1-28 ounce can tomato puree
1-28 ounce can tomato sauce
1 large onion, chopped
1-2 large garlic cloves, chopped
$\frac{1}{4}$ cup canola oil
$\frac{1}{2}$ cup sucanat
2 tablespoons molasses
1 teaspoon turmeric
1 teaspoon salt
2 tablespoons dried parsley
$\frac{1}{4}$ teaspoon crushed red pepper (optional)
2 tablespoons honey
2 tablespoons Bragg's Liquid Aminoes
$\frac{1}{2}$ cup fresh lemon juice
2-10 ounce jars Polaner Peach Fruit Spread
1-2 tablespoons Wright's liquid smoke

In a large sauce pan, sauté onions and garlic in oil. Add all other ingredients except lemon juice, peach fruit spread and liquid smoke. Cover and let simmer about 20 minutes. Add lemon juice, peach spread and liquid smoke. Let simmer another 15-20 minutes till flavors blend. Serve as you would any commercial barbecue sauce.

Yield: about 8-10 cups

YOUR FLAVA HOMEMADE GLUTEN

Gluten is the protein of wheat and is prepared as follows:

1. To 8 cups hard-wheat flour (high gluten content) add slowly 3-4 cups cold water, and mix into a stiff dough as for bread

2. Knead well, 8-10 minutes by the clock; or if you prefer to count the strokes count 450-500. Kneading develops the gluten and is very important.

3. Cover the dough ball with cold water and let stand for any convenient length of time – $\frac{1}{2}$ hour to overnight. This loosens the starch.

4. Now, wash out the starch by kneading the dough under water, renewing the water as necessary.

5. STOP washing just before the water is clear. You will notice that the dough is very soft as you wash it, then suddenly it becomes firm. THAT IS THE TIME TO STOP WASHING.

6. Rinse in clear water and place gluten on a board to drain.

7. Form into a roll and cut with a sharp knife into $\frac{1}{2}$ inch slices **OR** pull apart into irregularly shaped pieces.

8. Drop into a prepared meat flavored broth and cook, reducing heat low enough to keep gluten boiling gently, about $1\frac{1}{2}$ hours

9. When cooled, prepare as you would any other commercially prepared vege-gluten.

Recipe for broth follows on next page

MEAT FLAVORED BROTH FOR GLUTEN

In a small amount of oil, sauté onion, bell pepper, celery and garlic. Add about, 4-6 cups water and season with your favorite seasonings.

For Chicken Gluten use McKay's Chicken Seasoning

For Beef/Choplet Gluten use either or a combination of McKay's Beef Seasoning, Bragg's Aminoes, or Kitchen Bouquet Browning/Seasoning Sauce

For Fish Gluten use Kelp and McKay's Chicken Seasoning

Add other of your favorite seasonings/herbs as you like. Add slowly **BECAUSE YOU CAN'T TAKE IT OUT!!!!!!!**

(My students curried their gluten OR seasoned in the traditional Haitian stew meat way.)

Yield: depending on the size you make you could get up to 60 pieces of gluten.

You can also use instant gluten, which is available at most grocery and health food stores. Follow directions on label for making it into gluten.

"TOFU" Fish Sticks

1 lb. firm, water-packed tofu that has been frozen and thawed

Bragg's Liquid Aminoes – about $\frac{1}{4}$ - 1/3 cup

1 cup yellow cornmeal

1 teaspoon dried basil or parsley, or more to taste

$\frac{1}{2}$ - 1 teaspoon kelp powder

your favorite seasonings

Freeze tofu for at least 72 hours. Thaw and slice into fillets or strips or nuggets. Place in a dish and squirt with Bragg's Liquid Aminoes. Let marinate for about 30 minutes. In a bowl mix corn meal, basil, kelp and any other seasonings you would use to season fish. Dip marinated tofu into seasoned corn meal mixture and fry in canola oil OR bake in oven at 400° in a baking dish that has been sprayed with vegetable oil until golden brown, turning once. Serve with tartar sauce.

Yield: 4-6 fillets or about 14-16 sticks

Bermuda Curried Chicken
3-4 cups your favorite veggie chicken
2 tablespoons olive oil
1 onion, chopped
2 large cloves garlic, chopped
1 tablespoon, minced ginger root or more to taste
2 tablespoons mild curry powder or more to taste
2 tablespoons flour
1 5.5 ounce can premium coconut milk
2 cups water, more if desired
McKay's Chicken Style Seasoning to Taste

In a heavy skillet, brown the veggie chicken in olive oil. Set aside. In remaining olive oil sauté the onions and garlic until golden. Add the ginger root, curry powder and flour and stir well. Slowly stir in the coconut milk and water. Season to taste with McKay's Chicken Style. Add the browned veggie chicken. Cover and simmer for about 20 minutes to allow broth to thicken and flavors to develop. Adjust seasonings if necessary. Serve with rice.
Variation: Add one peeled, diced apple with the ginger root, curry powder and flour.

Serves 6

Jamaican Curry Chicken

12-14 Veggie Chicken Drumsticks (Oriental Brand)
4 tablespoons olive oil
1 onion chopped
1 small green pepper, chopped
2 large garlic cloves, chopped
1 tablespoons minced ginger root or more to taste
3 tablespoons mild curry powder or more to taste
1 sprig of thyme
1-14 ounce can premium coconut milk
2 cups water, more if desired
McKay's Chicken Style Seasoning

Pour oil into a heavy skillet. Brown the veggie drumsticks and set aside. In remaining oil, sauté the onions, peppers and garlic. Add ginger root, thyme and curry powder and stir well. Slowly add the coconut milk and water. Season to taste with McKay's Chicken Style. Add browned veggie drumsticks back to sauce. Cover and simmer about 20 minutes. ENJOY!!!!

Serves 6-8

Roti

2 cups all purpose, unbleached flour
1 1/3 cup whole wheat pastry flour
1 heaping teaspoon baking powder
1 teaspoon salt
2 tablespoons canola or olive oil
$\frac{1}{2}$ cup water

Sift dry ingredients into a bowl. Add oil and enough water to make a dough that is not too dry. Allow to rest for about 30 minutes. Cut dough into eight equal pieces and form into balls. Let dough rest again for about 2 minutes. On a floured board, roll dough balls into 6-8 inch disks. Heat a griddle (preferably cast iron) over medium heat. When hot, brush the griddle with oil. Then brush the pastry disks with oil on both sides. Place on hot griddle and cook until top starts to blister. Flip roti and cook for one minute more on the other side. Serve warm with your favorite curry.

Serves 4-8

Shirley's Big Ole Pot o' Gumbo

1 cup celery, chopped
1 cup red onion, chopped
1 cup green pepper, chopped
6 cloves garlic, chopped
1/3 cup fresh parsley, chopped
2 cups fresh sliced okra
½ cup green onions
2 – 4 ounce cans Old El Paso mild, green chiles
½ teaspoon (more) ground bay leaves
1 teaspoon thyme
1 teaspoon basil
1 teaspoon kelp powder
½ teaspoon salt
1 teaspoon NO MSG McKay's Chicken Style Seasoning
½ cup flour browned OR 2 tablespoons file' powder
1/3 cup canola oil
3-4 large tomatoes, crushed
1 cup veggie ham, diced
2-3 cups veggie sausage links, cut in half
2-3 cups veggie sausage
2-3 cups veggie chicken, broken into pieces
Water as needed

Saute' chopped vegetables in oil until tender. Add flour seasonings and continue sautéing for about three minutes. (If using file powder, omit flour. Add file powder at the end of cooking). Add 1 cup water, tomatoes, veggie-meat, chilies and okra. Bring to a boil, simmer 15-30 minutes. Add more water if necessary. Adjust seasonings to taste. Put gumbo into serving bowls and heap a serving of rice into the center of the gumbo. Yum, yum, eat 'em up!!

Variation: Add 1-cup fresh corn.
Serves 8-10

Pecan Patties

1 small onion, diced
½ small green bell pepper, diced
½ small red bell pepper, diced
Olive oil
2 cups pecan meal
3-4 slices whole wheat bread, cubed
1-2 tablespoons gluten flour
¼ to ½ cup nutritional yeast flakes
McKay's NO MSG Chicken style seasoning, to taste
Parsley, sage, savory, garlic, Jamaican allspice, Bragg's liquid aminoes to taste
Soy milk – enough to hold patties together

Sauté onions and bell pepper in olive oil. In a mixing bowl, add sautéed veggies to pecan meal, cubed whole wheat bread and gluten flour. Add yeast flakes and stir. Add chicken-style seasoning and other seasonings to taste. Add milk slowly until mixture is slightly stiff and able to be shaped into patties. Shape into patties and place on oil-sprayed baking pan. Bake in oven at 350-400 degrees until brown. Turn once.

Yield: about 12-18 patties

MENU IDEAS

BREAKFAST
Fruit Smoothie and Blueberry Muffins

LUNCH
Salad
Scalloped Potatoes
Honey Glazed Carrots   Savory Broccoli

SUPPER
Popcorn
Virgin Strawberry Daiquiri

For More Ideas
Log onto our website
www.stillshoutin.com

EAT YOUR
VEGGIES

Callaloo and Okra

3 pounds callaloo, chopped (or use fresh spinach)
6 medium okra, chopped
1 medium onion, chopped
1 medium tomato, diced
1 small green pepper, chopped
1 small red pepper, chopped
1 teaspoon canola or olive oil

Steam callaloo and okra in a small amount of water until done. While steaming sauté vegetables in oil. Combine both mixtures. Cover and let simmer about 10-15 minutes.

Optional seasonings: salt, McKay's NO MSG Chicken Style, garlic powder

Serves 6-8

Okra, Corn, Tomatoes

2 tablespoons olive oil
1 large onion, thinly sliced into rounds
2 bay leaves
$\frac{1}{2}$ teaspoon each thyme and basil
1 large green bell pepper, seeded and finely diced
3 large, fresh, vine-ripened tomatoes, chopped
2 cups fresh corn (frozen will also do)
2 cups small okra pods, left whole or cut into $\frac{1}{4}$ inch rounds
$\frac{1}{2}$ cup water
Salt, McKay's NO MISG Chicken Style Seasoning to taste

In a large iron skillet or heavy pan, heat olive oil and add onions, bay leaves thyme and basil. Sauté; and stir until onions are limp. Add bell pepper and continue cooking until onions are translucent. Add tomatoes, okra water and seasonings. Reduce heat to low and simmer uncovered for 15 minutes, stirring occasionally. Add corn and cook 5 minutes longer. Taste, adjusting seasoning if needed. Serve hot in a bowl with cornbread or over brown rice.

Serves 6

Stir-Fried Okra

3 tablespoons canola or olive oil
1 pound fresh okra, sliced
1 large onion, finely chopped
1 large green bell pepper, finely chopped
1 cup celery, finely chopped
$\frac{1}{4}$ teaspoon salt
$\frac{1}{2}$ teaspoon dried thyme
2-3 teaspoons Bragg's liquid aminoes (optional)

Place oil in a large skillet or wok over medium-high heat. Add okra and next 5 ingredients. Stir-fry mixture for 8-10 minutes or until okra is crisp-tender. Add optional Bragg's, stir constantly, cooking another 2 minutes or until okra is tender.

Variation: add red or yellow bell pepper, summer squash, veggie meat of your choice.

Serves 6

Vegetable Medley

1 cup fresh broccoli flowerettes, chopped
1 cup carrots, sliced diagonally
3 tablespoons olive oil
4 cups zucchini, or yellow crookneck squash, thinly sliced
1 medium green, red or yellow pepper, cut into 1 inch pieces
½ cup green onion, sliced
1 clove garlic, minced
2 medium tomatoes, cut into wedges
2 teaspoons fresh dillweed, snipped OR ½ teaspoon dried dillweed

In a large skillet cook broccoli and carrots in hot oil 3-4 minutes, or until crisp tender, stirring constantly. add squash, green pepper, onion and garlic. Cook covered over medium heat 5 minutes or more, or until squash and green pepper are crisp-tender, stirring constantly. Add tomatoes and dillweed. Cook uncovered 2-3 minutes more until heated through. Season to taste with optional salt.

Serves 8

Zucchini Patties

1 cup tofu mayonnaise
2 cups bread crumbs
3 cups shredded zucchini
1 teaspoon onion powder
1 teaspoon garlic powder
1 teaspoon salt
1/8 teaspoon tarragon
1/8 teaspoon marjoram
1/8 teaspoon thyme
1/8 teaspoon ground celery leaves
1/8 teaspoon ground bay leaves

Mix all ingredients, varying the seasonings according to taste. Shape mixture into patties an brown them in a pan that has been sprayed with vegetable spray.

Yield 12 patties

Harvard Beets

2 teaspoons cornstarch
$\frac{3}{4}$ cup date sugar
$\frac{1}{2}$ fresh cup lemon juice
4 large beets, sliced
Mix cornstarch, sugar and lemon juice in saucepan. Add beets and steam until tender. Add optional salt, to taste, if desired.

Serves 6

Scrumptious Squash Casserole
1 large yellow squash OR 4-5 cups yellow squash, diced
1 medium onion, chopped
$\frac{1}{4}$ cup soy mayonnaise
$\frac{1}{4}$ cup soy sour cream
1 cup cracker or bread crumbs
1 package soy cheddar or Monterey jack cheese, shredded
Your favorite seasonings to taste – salt, McKay's Chicken
Style, herbs

Bring a small amount of water to a boil in a large pan. Add
squash and onions, return to boil, then lower heat and cook
until crisp tender. Drain liquid into a heatproof container.
Add other ingredients to cooked squash mixture saving some
of the cheese for the top of the casserole. Add some of the
liquid back to the casserole mixture to make it smooth and
easy to stir. Add your favorite seasonings and adjust to
taste. Pour into a casserole dish that has been sprayed with
vegetable spray. Sprinkle the rest of the cheese on top of
the casserole. Cover casserole and bake in 350° oven until
heated thoroughly and cheese is nice and bubbly. (I have
noticed that soy cheese hardens when it is baked unless you
cover it.) I have so missed squash casserole and the
traditional one is full of animal fat and cholesterol. This is
the closest I have ever gotten and it is great. It is
cholesterol-free and has a soufflé like texture. It always
goes fast at our cooking classes.

Serves 8-10

King Cole Curry

1 small bunch broccoli, cut into florets
½ head cauliflower, cut into florets
1 medium boiling potato, quartered and sliced
½ medium onion, chopped
2 tablespoons whole wheat flour
1 teaspoon turmeric
1 tablespoon mild curry
¾ cup tofu, drained and rinsed
3 tablespoon fresh lemon juice
1 tablespoon nutritional yeast flakes
½ cup plain bread crumbs
½ teaspoon paprika
½ teaspoon Italian seasoning
½ tablespoon salt
Vegetable cooking spray

Preheat the oven to 350°F. Separately steam the broccoli, cauliflower and potato until tender but firm. While the vegetables steam, make the sauce—coat a large heavy skillet with the cooking spray. Add onion and cook over moderate heat for 2 minutes. Add flour and turmeric and curry; cook stirring until the color is evenly distributed. Pour in 1 cup cold water, continuing to stir until the mixture thickens, 2-3 minutes. Blend tofu,, lemon juice, yeast flakes and ½ cup cold water until smooth and add to sauce mixture. Spread half the vegetables in a medium baking pan. Top with half the tofu sauce. Add the remaining vegetables and top with remaining sauce. In a small bowl, mix bread crumbs and Italian seasoning. Sprinkle mixture evenly over the top of casserole. Cover, bake 10 minutes. Uncover and bake 10-15 minutes more.

Serves 6-8

Curried Potatoes

Olive Oil
1 medium onion, chopped
1-2 pounds potatoes, peeled and diced
3 tablespoons curry powder
1-1/2 cups water
Season to taste with salt, garlic powder, Pepper-like
seasoning, thyme
Optional: add one can garbanzo beans, drained

Heat oil in large sauce pan and sauté onions in small amount of
olive oil. Add potatoes and other ingredients, stirring to coat
potatoes well. Add water; cover and let simmer until
potatoes are tender. (Serve in the roti!!!)

Serves 6-8

Jackie's Skillet Potatoes

2-3 tablespoons olive oil
4 -6 medium potatoes, thinly sliced
1 large onion, thinly sliced and separated into rings
2-3 garlic cloves, chopped
1-1 ½ cups your favorite soy cheddar cheese, grated
½ cup chives (save some for topping)
Salt
Pepper-like Seasoning

Heat oil in a large skillet. Take pan off heat and cover the bottom of the pan with a layer of potatoes, onion, garlic, cheese, chives, salt and pepper-like seasoning. Keep layering, ending with cheese. Cover and cook on low heat for about 30 minutes or until the potatoes and onions are tender. Remove cover and place in oven under broiler. Broil till desired brownness. Garnish with chives. Slice and serve!!

Serves 6-8

I get my hair done every Friday at Tiffani's Hair Studio with my friends Jackie and Karnice. After "catching up" Jackie and I cannot leave until we exchange recipe ideas. Here is one of my favorites…..her daddy made sure her mom got the recipe!!!!! Enjoy!!

Mr. Knowles Scrumptious Squash & Green Tomatoes

Olive oil
4 medium yellow squash
2 small green tomato, sliced
½ onion, chopped
water
Salt or McKay's NO MSG Chicken style seasoning to taste

Place a small amount of olive oil in a cast-iron skillet. Heat and add ½ the squash, searing. Add rest of squash, green tomato and onion, stirring constantly. Reduce to low heat, add a little water, cover and steam till desired tenderness. Season to taste.

Serves 6

I met Mr. Knowles while I was conducting a cooking class at Wildwood Lifestyle Center and Hospital. A southern gentlemen, he enjoyed the dishes I demonstrated. He could not believe, however, that I had not tasted squash and green tomatoes. Here is his recipe. I make it with food out of our garden.

Steamed Cabbage

Olive oil
1 medium onion, sliced
$\frac{1}{2}$ large green pepper, sliced
2 tablespoons McKay's NO MSG Chicken Style Seasoning
2 tablespoons BAKON
1 cup water
1 medium head cabbage, shredded

Sauté onion and bell pepper in small amount of olive oil. Add chicken like seasoning and bacon-like seasoning and stir. Add water and bring to boil. Stir in cabbage and bring back to boil. (add more water if necessary). Reduce heat and simmer UNCOVERED until desired tenderness is reached. Covering the cabbage will darken it.
Serves 8-10

Savory Broccoli

Olive oil
1 medium onion, chopped
2-3 cloves garlic, chopped
6-8 cups fresh, chopped broccoli
Water
McKay's NO MSG Chicken Style Seasoning

In a large saucepan, sauté onion and garlic. Stir in broccoli. Add enough water to keep broccoli from sticking to pan, about $\frac{1}{2}$ - 1 cup. Bring to boil. Reduce heat and simmer UNCOVERED! Until desired tenderness is reached. Season to taste with chicken like seasoning.

Serves 6-8

Southern Collards

Olive oil
1 medium onion, finely chopped
2-3 garlic cloves, sliced
2-3 tablespons McKay's NO MSG chicken like seasoning
$\frac{1}{4}$ cup BAKON to taste (optional)
2 pounds collard greens
1-2 cups water

Sort and wash collards. Strip leaves from stalks and thinly
cut. In large pot, heat some olive oil. Saute the onions until
lightly browned. Add garlic and stir fry one to two minutes.
Add about $\frac{1}{4}$ cup bacon seasoning and 2-3 tablespoons
chicken like seasoning. Add water and bring to boil. Start
adding greens, stirring down. As they begin to wilt add more
until all are in the pot. Mix well. Bring to boil, then reduce
heat and cook until greens reach desired tenderness.
(bacon like seasoning gives the greens that traditional, down-
home, smoked flavor). Adjust seasonings as necessary.

Serves 6-8

*I served these greens as samples at a Sisters Network
event in Atlanta in 1998. A lady from Ohio took the rest
of the BAKON I had home in a cup so she could make
them when she got back. Great to use in place of turkey
wings!! My girlfriend Deitra uses the Earth Balance
Natural Shortening in her greens!!!   Umm, umm, ummhh!!*

MENU IDEAS

BREAKFAST
Whole Grain Waffles with Strawberry Topping
Scrambled Tofu
Vege Sausage

LUNCH
Pigeon Peas and Rice
Bermuda Curried Vege Chicken
Steamed Cabbage
Easy Yeast Rolls

SUPPER
Macaroni Salad
Crackers

For More Ideas
Log onto our website
www.stillshoutin.com

SOUPS AND STEWS

Egyptian Stew

2 tablespoons olive oil
1 cup onion, sliced
½ cup green pepper, sliced
2 cups corn kernels
2 cups lima beans, cooked
1/3 cup tomatoes, fresh or canned
2 cups zucchini, sliced
½ cup fresh parsley, chopped

Saute' onions and green pepper in oil. Add corn and lima beans and cook on low heat for 15 minutes. Add tomatoes and zucchini and cook an additional 15 to 20 minutes. Add parsley just before serving.

Serves 8

Mexican Tortilla Soup

1 large onion, chopped
6 large garlic cloves, minced
2 tablespoons vegetable oil
1 teaspoon ground cumin
$\frac{1}{2}$ teaspoon dried oregano
4 cups chopped fresh tomatoes
3 cups vegetable stock
1/3 cup fresh lime juice
Salt to taste
Tortilla chips

Saute' onion and garlic in oil in a medium pot until onion is
clear. Add cumin and oregano and sauté for a few more
minutes. Add chopped tomatoes and salt to taste. Cover and
cook on low until tomatoes begin to soften, stirring
occasionally. Add vegetable stock and simmer, covered for
about 15 minutes. Add lime juice. Serve in bowls with
crumbled tortilla chips.

Serves 4

Cuban Black Beans

1 pound dry black beans
1 large onion, finely chopped
1 large green pepper, finely chopped
4 large cloves garlic, finely chopped
1 medium tomato, finely chopped
$1\frac{1}{2}$ teaspoons cumin, more if desired
1 teaspoon dried oregano
2 tablespoons olive oil
McKay's NO MSG Chicken Style Seasoning to taste
Salt to taste (optional)

Sort and wash beans. Place in a crockpot along with onion, green pepper, tomato, garlic, cumin and oregano. Add enough water till about 2 inches above the beans. Follow manufacturer's directions for cooking overnight or for 4 hours, adding more water if necessary. When beans are tender, add olive oil, Mckay's Chicken Style and optional salt to taste. Serve over yellow rice or in bowls with a dollop of soy sour cream topped with salsa and a slice of cornbread on the side!!

Variation: Add vege baco or ham bits near end of cooking.

Serves 8

Ground Nut Stew

My late brother Stephen, loved to add peanut butter to my mom's vegetable soup! We thought it was gross. Wouldn't you know, it's an African tradition!!

2 tablespoons vegetable oil
1 large onion, chopped
2 large cloves garlic, chopped
1 medium eggplant, chopped
10 small okra, sliced
6 ounce can of tomato paste
1 large tomato, chopped
½ cup peanut butter, or more to taste
½ teaspoon dried thyme
4-6 cups water
salt to taste
McKays Chicken Style Seasoning (optional)

In soup pot, sauté onion, garlic, eggplant and okra in oil. Add tomato paste, chopped tomato, peanut butter and thyme. Stir until heated and peanut butter and tomato paste soften. Add water slowly to get a soup consistency. Add salt and optional seasonings to taste. Cover and let simmer for about 30 minutes.
Variations: Add 2 cups vege chicken or vege steak. Add coco/eddoe. Season with two slices of fresh ginger.
Serves 6

Curried Lentil Soup

1 pound dry, lentils, sorted and rinsed (choose your color)
1 large carrot, diced
1 medium onion, chopped
1 medium potato, diced
3 cloves garlic, chopped
1 stalk celery, chopped
1 large tomato, diced
2 tablespoons mild curry powder
$\frac{1}{2}$ - 1 teaspoon powdered ginger
Water
Your favorite herbs, coriander. McKay's NO MSG Chicken Style Seasoning, to taste. . Optional salt to taste. Optional oil to taste. Optional coconut milk, YUM!!

In a large pot place beans, vegetables and seasonings. Add enough water till about 2 inches above the beans. Bring to a boil. Reduce heat and simmer until beans are tender, about 45 minutes to an hour, adding more water if necessary. Adjust seasonings and add optional oil and salt.

Serves 10-12

Crockpot Chik'n Stew

1 cup raw cashews, rinsed
1 tablespoon cornstarch
6 cups water or more if needed
1 small onion, chopped
1 stalk celery, chopped
½ medium red pepper, chopped
1 16-ounce bag mixed vegetables
1 cup your favorite veggie chicken, chopped
1 medium potato, peeled and diced
1 cup broccoli flowerettes
Season to taste with McKay's NO MSG Chicken Style
Seasoning, garlic powder, basil and *cardamom*-replaces
nutmeg.

Place cashews and cornstarch in blender with one cup of
water and blend until smooth. Add more water if necessary.
While nuts are blending, place veggie meat and all veggies
except broccoli into crockpot. Add blended nuts, and rest of
water to crockpot. Turn to high and let cook for about two
hours. Add seasonings adjusting to taste. Let cook another
two hours and then check for doneness of veggies. When
about ready add broccoli and cook for another 15 minutes
so broccoli won't turn that awful green color. Dish up and
serve with salad and rolls or cornbread.

VARIATION: Add all ingredients to crockpot except
broccoli and cook on low setting overnight. Add broccoli and
adjust seasonings about 15 minutes before serving

MENU IDEAS

BREAKFAST
Breakfast Hash
Applesauce
Angel Biscuits

LUNCH
Salad
Lasagne
Kernel Corn
Garlic Bread

SUPPER
Seasonal Fruit Salad

For More Ideas
Log onto our website
www.stillshoutin.com

SAUCES, SALADS, SPREADS AND SUCH

Guacamole

4 medium ripe avocadoes
1 container your favorite soy sour cream
1 medium tomato, diced
1 medium onion, finely chopped
juice of one lemon
juice of one lime
Salt to taste

Peel and mash avocadoes. Add other ingredients and mix
well. Add salt to taste. Serve with peach salsa and tortilla
chips as appetizer/party food or with nachos.
Yield: 6 cups

Peach Salsa

1 16-ounce jar On the Border Salsa, medium flavor, (it's
vinegar-free)
1/3 can Welch's white grape peach juice, thawed

Mix ingredients together and serve with guacamole and
tortilla chips as appetizer/party food or over nachos. Our
family loves this!!
Yield: about 2½ cups

Fresh Salsa

4 cups chopped fresh tomatoes
1 onion, chopped
½ cup chopped green bell pepper
1 - 4 ounce can diced green chilies
¼ cup chopped fresh parsley
2 tablespoons fresh cilantro
1 ½ tablespoons fresh lemon juice
2 cloves garlic, minced
¼ teaspoon ground cumin
¼ teaspoon ground oregano
Salt to taste (optional)

Combine all ingredients and mix well. Refrigerate for a few hours to overnight to let flavors blend.

Servings 16

Garlic Spread for Garlic Bread

½ cup olive oil
1 tablespoon basil
1 tablespoon garlic powder (3-4 cloves fresh, chopped garlic works well too)
2 tablespoons nutritional yeast flakes (adds cheesy flavor)

In a small bowl, mix olive oil, basil, garlic and nutritional yeast flakes. Mixture should be easy to spread. Adjust ingredients for taste and consistency and spread on bread. Bake in oven to desired crispness.

Makes about ¾ cup

Better Butter

1/3 cup corn meal mush (1/2 cup fine cornmeal cooked in 1 cup water)

¼ cup water

½ cup raw cashew pieces, washed

¾ teaspoon salt

1/3 cup coconut milk

1 teaspoon non-alcoholic butter flavoring

Whiz cashews and water in blender until VERY smooth. (If necessary to keep the ingredients blending until the cashews are smooth, add the coconut milk.) Add remaining ingredients and continue blending until smooth. Refrigerate.

Yield: 1 pint – 32 servings

We served this to lifestyle guests who were trying to reverse diabetes and its complications. Many of them really enjoyed it.

Cheez Sauce

2 cups water
$\frac{1}{4}$ cup clean raw cashews
1 - 4 ounce jar pimientos
$\frac{1}{2}$ - 1 cup nutritional yeast flakes (secret for cheesy taste)
1 $\frac{1}{2}$ tablespoon cornstarch
1 tablespoon fresh lemon juice
1 $\frac{1}{2}$ teaspoon salt
$\frac{1}{2}$ teaspoon onion powder
$\frac{1}{4}$ teaspoon garlic powder

Blend cashews in about $\frac{1}{2}$ cup of the water until very smooth. Add remaining water and other ingredients and continue blending until smooth. Simmer in a heavy saucepan until thickened, stirring constantly, 5-6 minutes.
Serves 12

VARIATION: Add $\frac{1}{2}$ teaspoon cumin, about $\frac{1}{2}$ cup of your favorite vegetarian beef or sausage, and your favorite salsa to the cheez sauce for a sensational dip! Serve with tortilla chips

Soy Mayonnaise

1 package soft or firm silken tofu
2 Tablespoons plus 2 teaspoons lemon juice
6 T. oil
1 $\frac{1}{2}$ Tablespoons honey
$\frac{3}{4}$ teaspoon salt

In blender or food processor, combine all ingredients and process for one minute or until smooth. Refrigerate until serving time. Use within 7-10 days.
Yield: 2 cups

Spinach Dip

1 10 ounce package frozen spinach, chopped
1 pkg. Knorr vegetable soup mix
2 cups your favorite soy sour cream
½ -1 cup your favorite soy mayonnaise
Optional ingredients: 1/2 cup each of chopped green onions,
red bell pepper, water chestnuts.

Thaw and squeeze spinach dry. Mix spinach and other
ingredients together in a bowl. Cover and refrigerate for at
least 2 hours before serving. Serve as a dip with crackers.
Another delicious serving suggestion is to carve out the
center of a round loaf of unsliced, whole grain bread. Place
dip in the "bowl" of the bread. Place on a serving tray. Tear
carved out piece into smaller dipping pieces and place around
the loaf. Guests can use the torn pieces as dippers. This is
one recipe I learned to love some 25 years ago. You don't
have the guilt when you use healthier ingredients.

Yield: 4 cups

Variation: Add 1 small jar of artichokes, drained. Place in
oven proof dish, cover with soy mozzarella cheese, grated
and bake till heated through and cheese is melted. May also
broil till cheese browns lightly.

Thousand Island Salad Dressing

2 cups soy mayonnaise
1 - 8 ounce can tomato sauce
½ cup vinegar free, sweet pickle relish, more or less if desired
½ cup sliced, ripe green olives, more or less if desired
4 ounce jar pimento, diced
Salt (optional)

In a mixing bowl, gently stir all ingredients until thoroughly mixed. Adjust relish, olives and pimento to taste. Serve.

Yield: 4-5 cups

Avocado Salad Dressing

1 medium, ripe avocado
juice of one lemon and/or lime (depending on your preference, I use both)
1/3 cup water – or more to desired consistency
Honey and salt to taste (optional)

In a blender, place the peeled, sliced avocado. Add lemon and lime juices and water to make it thick, but pourable. Add optional honey and salt to taste. Serve.

Servings 16

Pam's Easy Creamy Italian Salad Dressing
1 package Good Seasons Italian Salad Dressing Mix
$\frac{1}{4}$ cup lemon juice
$\frac{3}{4}$ cup water
$\frac{1}{2}$ cup canola or olive oil
1 package of Mori-Nu Soft, Silken Tofu

In a blender place all ingredients. Blend until smooth. Add more water to make dressing pourable, if needed. Serve.

Serves 12

Creamy Herb Dip
1 package firm, silken tofu
3 tablespoons canola oil
2 tablespoons plus 1 teaspoon lemon juice
2 teaspoons plus honey to taste
$\frac{3}{4}$ teaspoon salt
2-3 tablespoons water
1-2 garlic cloves
2 tablespoons dried basil
2 teaspoons dried parsley
$\frac{1}{4}$ teaspoon dill

Blend all ingredients well, until smooth. Use as a topping for baked potatoes.

Serves 16

OPTIONAL: Use soft tofu instead for a pourable salad dressing.

Ranch-Like Dressing

1 cup buttermilk (plain soy milk with 1 T. lemon juice)
1 cup soy sour cream
½ cup soy mayonnaise
1 teaspoon salt
½ teaspoon Like Pepper seasoning
2 teaspoons onion powder
1 teaspoon garlic powder
2-3 tablespoons additional lemon juice
2-3 tablespoons dried parsley

Mix all ingredients together by stirring. Let sit a couple of hours for flavor to develop. Adjust seasonings as desired. Serve

Yield: about 3 cups

If too thin, add some silken tofu.

Like Raspberry Vinaigrette Dressing

¼ cup lemon juice
½ cup oil
½ - 1 can white grape raspberry concentrate (depending on your preference)
1 package Good Season's Italian salad dressing

Mix all ingredients well! Serve.

Fresh Collard Green Salad

2 cups raw, young tender collards, shredded
2 cups raw green cabbage, shredded
1 cup fresh parsley, chopped
½ medium red onion, chopped fine
1 medium tomato, chopped
Soy baco bits or Veggie Bacon cooked and broken into small pieces (optional)

In a medium bowl, mix collards, cabbage, parsley and onion. Pour in 1-2 cups of your favorite oil based salad dressing (use Like Raspberry Vinaigrette) let marinade 4 hours to overnight. Pour out marinade and place salad in serving bowl. Top with diced tomato and optional baco bits or veggie bacon.
Serves 6

Fresh Spinach Salad

½ pound fresh spinach cut in shreds
1 medium onion, minced
4 tablespoons diced celery
¼ cup scrambled tofu
½ teaspoon NO MSG Mckay's Chicken Style Seasoning
2 tablespoons soy baco bits (optional)

Toss and chill salad. Serve with dressing of your choice
Serves 8

(I have found that crumbling firm tofu and sprinkling some of it with turmeric, a little garlic powder and some McKay's Chicken style adds the appearance of boiled egg yolk to salads. Mix in some of the remaining unseasoned tofu for a complete boiled egg appearance.)

"Leftover" Black-eyed Pea and Corn Salad

2 cups leftover black-eyed peas, rinsed
2 cups leftover kernel corn, drained
½ cup red bell pepper, chopped
1 small red onion, chopped
2 tablespoons lemon juice (more or less, as desired)
1 tablespoon olive oil, optional
1 tablespoon fresh parsley, chopped
basil, garlic, salt to taste

Mix all ingredients in a bowl, adjusting to taste. Let marinate for several hours. Serve.
Serves 6

(I had often seen this salad but did not eat it because of the vinegar. I had some "leftovers" one day and ended up with this. Add seasonings carefully as the beans and corn should already be flavored. Canned veggies should work as well.)

Hummus

2 cups cooked or canned garbanzos, with liquid
1/3 cup fresh lemon juice
¼ cup tahini (sesame seed butter)
½ teaspoon salt
½ teaspoon onion powder
½ teaspoon cumin, or to taste
2 cloves garlic
McKay's No MSG Chicken Style Seasoning to taste (optional)

Blend all ingredients until smooth and creamy. Refrigerate. Delicious on pita bread with lettuce, tomato, bean sprouts.

Yield: about 3 cups

Tofu Egg Salad(s)

1 one-pound tub of water packed tofu, firm or extra firm
1 small onion, finely chopped
1 tablespoon or more McKay's NO MSG chicken style seasoning
$\frac{1}{4}$ teaspoon or more turmeric
$\frac{1}{2}$ small red pepper, finely chopped
6-8 ripe, green olives, chopped
1 stalk celery, finely chopped
Pa's pickle relish to taste
1 teaspoon or more Bragg's Aminos
$\frac{1}{2}$ cup or more your favorite mayonnaise

Cut tofu into several large pieces, place in colander and let drain for at least ten minutes. Place drained tofu into a mixing bowl and mash to consistency of egg salad. Add other ingredients, adjusting for taste as necessary. Serve on sandwiches or as appetizer/party food with vegetables or crackers.

Yield: about 4 cups

Variation: My friend Carol makes hers without the pickle relish and to the other ingredients adds $\frac{1}{2}$ stalk minced celery, $\frac{1}{2}$ chopped green pepper, $\frac{1}{2}$ chopped red pepper, $\frac{1}{2}$ teaspoon curry powder or coriander.

Chicken Salad

4 cups your favorite veggie chicken, grated
1 medium onion, finely chopped
1 stalk celery, chopped
½ cup or more of Pa's vinegar-free pickle relish
1 cup your favorite soy mayonnaise, more or less if needed
Garlic powder and McKay's No MSG Chicken Style Seasoning to taste

Mix all ingredients together. Chill to let flavors blend. Serve with crackers or make into finger sandwiches on various whole grain breads. Serve.

Variation: Use veggie hot dogs, veggie ham, or veggie turkey as the base meat and season the same or experiment with your own favorite seasonings.

Yield: about 6 cups

Fruit Dip

3 containers Tofutti Better than Cream Cheese, plain
1 container Tofutti Better Than Sour Cream, plain
1 cup evaporated cane juice sugar
1 tablespoon alcohol-free almond flavoring

Mix ingredients well. Chill. Serve with fresh fruit tray.

MENU IDEAS

BREAKFAST
Grits and Scrambled Tofu
Wheat Toast or Biscuits
Fruit Salad

LUNCH
Black-eyed Peas and Brown Rice
Baked Sweet Potato
Southern Collards and Cornbread

SUPPER
Nacho Cheez Dip
Tortilla Chips

For More Ideas
Log onto our website
www.stillshoutin.com

FAVORITE
BREADS

Southern Cornbread

1 ½ cups yellow or white whole grain cornmeal

½ cup yellow or white whole grain grits

½ cup whole wheat pastry flour

2 tablespoons sweetener (optional)

1 teaspoon salt

4 teaspoons Featherweight baking powder

1 tablespoon EnerG egg replacer

1 ¾ cups vanilla flavored soy milk

2 tablespoons canola oil

hot water

vegetable oil spray.

Heat oven to 400 degrees. Spray an iron skillet with vegetable spray and place in oven to heat. Measure all dry ingredients into a mixing bowl. Mix all liquid ingredients together. Add all at once to dry ingredients. Stir, adding enough hot water to make a smooth batter. Remove skillet from oven. Pour cornbread batter into pan immediately (secret to great crust). Place in oven and bake until done.

Variations: Add corn and bell peppers or mild chilies to the batter. Add 1 heaping tablespoon of soy sour cream and 1 tablespoon honey to batter. Add some crumbled veggie bacon to batter.

Serves 8
Makes about 18 muffins

Easy Yeast Rolls

1 cup boiling water
½ cup Earth Balance margarine
1/3 cup natural sugar
1 package yeast
1 tablespoon EnerG Egg Replacer dissolved in 1/3 cup water
1 teaspoon salt
2 cups whole wheat pastry flour
1 cup all-purpose, unbleached flour

In a medium pot, pour water and bring to boil. Take off heat and add margarine to melt. Mix flours together, sift and set aside. When the margarine has melted, add sugar. When liquid has cooled to lukewarm, add yeast and stir until dissolved. Add powdered egg replacer mixture and salt to liquid. Sift mixed flours into liquid, about ¾ cup at a time. Continue adding flour just until you have a soft dough. Cover and let rise or place into refrigerator until ready to use. Make rolls. Let rise. Bake in 400° oven until golden brown, about 15 minutes. Serve.

Yield: 2 dozen rolls

Roti

2 cups all purpose, unbleached flour
1 1/3 cup whole wheat pastry flour
1 heaping teaspoon Featherweight baking powder
1 teaspoon salt
2 tablespoons canola or olive oil
½ cup water

Sift dry ingredients into a bowl. Add oil and enough water to make a dough that is not too dry. Allow to rest for about 30 minutes. Cut dough into eight equal pieces and form into balls. Let dough rest again for about 2 minutes. On a floured board, roll dough balls into 6-8 inch disks. Heat a griddle (preferably cast iron) over medium heat. When hot, brush the griddle with oil. Then brush the pastry disks with oil on both sides. Place on hot griddle and cook until top starts to blister. Flip roti and cook for one minute more on the other side. Serve warm with your favorite curry.

Yield: 6-8 roti

Barbadon Coocoo

2 ¼ cups water
10 small okra, finely sliced
¼ red bell pepper, finely chopped
1 teaspoon salt
1 tablespoon soy margarine
1 cup cornmeal-fine or gritty

In a medium pot, boil the okra, bell pepper, and salt. When mixture thickens, remove half of it and set aside. Stir in margarine and reduce to low heat. SLOWLY add the corn meal, stirring constantly with a wooden spoon. As this mixture thickens, add the rest of the okra mixture. Keep stirring, adding more water slowly if needed. Let simmer over low heat for about 15 more minutes. The final mixture should look like smooth mashed potatoes.   I have heard that if you mound the final mixture in a bowl and add gravy....umm, umm, umm!!
Serves 4

My friends Anthony and Carol Pierre introduced this to me!! Love It!! They became vegetarians and eat it now with veggie fish.

HoeCake

The following narrative from an unknown slave advised this method for making HOE CAKES:

Stand in the shade near the edge of the field. Light a fire from whatever brush and twigs there may be. On the greased side of the blade of your hoe, mix meal and water until it is thick enough to fry. Add salt, if you remembered to bring any! Lean the hoe into the fire until the top side of the bread bubbles. Flip it and brown the other side. (If you do it without a hoe, make suitable changes in the kitchen.) My Great Gramma Lula used to make hoe cake in one piece in a skillet and serve with molasses. Here are two recipes that I now use.

Recipe #1

1 cup corn meal
$\frac{1}{2}$ teaspoon salt
1 teaspoon sugar
$\frac{3}{4}$ - 1 cup boiling water

Mix all ingredients thoroughly. Drop by tablespoonful in a small amount of oil on a griddle or skillet. Cook until brown, flip and brown other side.

Yield: about 8-10

Recipe #2

1 cup buttermilk (plain soy milk with 1 T. lemon juice)
1 cup whole grain cornmeal
1 cup white whole wheat flour
1 tablespoon EnerG egg replacer
1 tablespoon sugar
1 teaspoon Featherweight baking powder, heaping
2 teaspoons canola oil
Water as needed to thin batter

Mix all ingredients. Drop batter by tablespoonful in a small amount of oil on a griddle or skillet. Cook until brown, flip and brown other side.

Yield: about a dozen

MENU IDEAS

BREAKFAST
Granola with Banana
Bagel with soy Cream Cheese and
Strawberry Fruit Spread

LUNCH
Stir-fried Veggies
Brown Rice

SUPPER
Sub Sandwiches with Vege Slices
Peach or Strawberry Sorbet

For More Ideas
Log onto our website
www.stillshoutin.com

SWEET ENDINGS

Fruity Parfait

1 package Mori-Nu Vanilla Pudding Mix
1 package Mori-Nu silken tofu
$\frac{1}{2}$ container your favorite soy cream cheese
Your favorite soy, nut or rice milk
2 cups raspberries and 2 cups blueberries OR 4 cups one type of fruit
SOY Whipped Cream Topping

Place pudding mix, tofu, and cream cheese in blender. Add enough soy milk to blend until smooth. In a clear glass bowl spoon pudding, then blueberries, more pudding, then raspberries (or other fruit as desired), ending with fruit. Top with Soy Whipped Cream Topping and garnish with coconut, your favorite cookie crumbs or granola. Chill and serve.
Variation:
 Place in individual parfait glasses.
Begin layering in bowl with your favorite cookie or granola.
Use soy yogurt instead of pudding.

Makes 4 servings

Rwanda's Simple Peach Sorbet

5 cups frozen peaches
2-12 ounce cans white grape peach juice concentrate, thawed

Place ingredients in blender or food processor and blend until smooth. Scoop into serving dishes and serve.

Serves 6-8

Strawberry Mousse
1/3 cup soy milk
1 package Mori-Nu silken tofu, firm or extra firm
1 package Mori-Nu Mates Vanilla Pudding/Pie Mix
1 cup fresh or frozen strawberries

Blend or food process all ingredients until smooth. You may need to add some more soy milk or water to make ingredients blend more smoothly. This will also ensure a light, mousse texture.   Spoon into serving cups and serve.

Variation: use other favorite fruits or carob chips in place of strawberries.

Serves 4-6

Rwanda's Magnificent Carob Mousse
1 package Mori-Nu Silken Tofu, firm
1 package Mori-Nu Pudding Mix
1 cup carob chips, or more to taste
1 tablespoon Roma
Your favorite vanilla soy milk

Place first four ingredients in a blender. Add enough soy milk to blend easily. Continue blending and adding milk to desired consistency. Place into dessert cups and chill until time to serve.

Serves 4-6

Rwanda Wynder is a Godsend. She worked in our ministry and along with my mom, she and I worked on creating dishes for our lifestyle guests. We had so much fun creating these sorbet and mousse recipes. They are soooooo good and easy!! Thanks Rwanda!!

Eddie's Favorite Banana Pudding

1 package Vanilla Mori-Nu Pudding mix
1 package Mori Nu firm, silken tofu
3-4 medium bananas
1 bag Mi-Del vanilla wafers
Vanilla soy milk

Mix pudding mix with tofu according to directions on package, using your favorite brand of vanilla soy milk to make it blendable and easy to spread.   In the bottom and sides of an 8x8 baking dish, place a layer of vanilla wafers. Layer half the sliced bananas and half the pudding.   Repeat again, ending with pudding. Top with crushed vanilla wafers or chopped coconut. Refrigerate.

Variations: Add 1 teaspoon of banana OR coconut alcohol-free flavoring to pudding.   Use Mi-Del Ginger Snaps in place of vanilla wafers. (My husband Eddie loves to eat it for breakfast!)

My husband loves this. We eat it for breakfast. Sampled this at a health event at Morehouse School of Medicine. Then president James Gavin, III, MD couldn't stop eating it.

Tofu Cheesecake with Peach Mango Topping

1 cup evaporated cane juice crystals

3 containers Tofutti Better Than Cream Cheese

1 box extra firm Mori-Nu silken tofu

2 tablespoons EnerG egg replacer

$\frac{1}{2}$ cup water

1 tablespoon lemon juice

1 tablespoon vanilla flavoring

$\frac{1}{2}$ teaspoon salt

2-3 tablespoons cornstarch

Lemon zest to taste (optional)

Blend or food process all ingredients until smooth. Pour blended ingredients into prepared pie crust and bake at 350° for 30 minutes, then reduce oven to 250° and bake for 20-30 minutes till inserted toothpick comes out clean. Chill. Cover/serve with peach/mango topping.

Peach/Mango Topping

1 - 12 ounce can white grape peach juice concentrate
1 heaping tablespoon cornstarch
1 cup peeled peaches, diced large
1 cup mango, diced large

Pour fruit juice and cornstarch into small pot. Heat until thickened, stirring constantly. Remove from heat and let cool. Add fruit and stir. Top entire cheesecake or by slice. Experiment with other fruits and flavorings. This is also great on waffles for breakfast.

Yield: About 2 cups

Auntie Donna's Yum Yum Ice Cream

2 cups vanilla soy milk or soy creamer
1 cup sweetener
1 container Tofutti Better than Cream Cheese
1 package Mori Nu extra firm silken tofu
2 teaspoons vanilla flavoring

Mix all ingredients in blender until smooth. Pour into ice cream freezer and follow manufacturer's instructions.
Yield 1 ½ quarts

Variation: use SilkNog in place of vanilla milk!

Lisa's Luscious Pound Cake

3 cups unbleached flour (may mix unbleached and whole wheat pastry)
2 cups evaporated cane juice crystals or turbinado sugar
3 ½ teaspoons Featherweight Baking Powder, heaping
1 teaspoon salt
1½ cups your favorite soymilk, plain or vanilla
½ package Mori-Nu silken tofu, firm or extra-firm
2 tablespoons your favorite vanilla flavoring, alcohol-free
1 cup canola oil

Preheat oven to 350°. Mix dry ingredients together in a bowl. In a blender, blend together liquid ingredients and tofu. Slowly pour liquid mixture into dry mixture and gently stir together. Be careful not to over-mix. Batter will initially be coarse. Add **2 tablespoons of lemon juice** to the batter and stir again briefly. Batter will become smoother from lemon juice. Pour batter into prepared Bundt pan. Bake for 50 to 55 minutes or until a toothpick inserted in the center comes out clean. Cool for 30 to 45 minutes before applying frosting or glaze.

Yield: 20-24 servings

Variations:

For lemon pound cake add lemon flavoring and/or ½-1 teaspoon grated lemon peel to batter.

For vanilla cake use Very Vanilla Silk soymilk and add a drop of vanilla to glaze.

For carob cake use 1 $\frac{1}{2}$ cups turbinado and $\frac{1}{2}$ cup sucanat; 2 $\frac{3}{4}$ cup flour and $\frac{1}{2}$ cup carob powder; 1-2 tablespoons of Roma, silk vanilla creamer.

For other tastes, experiment with other flavorings. Almond is great.

Add $\frac{1}{4}$ cup more soy milk and spoon into cupcake cups.
Makes about 24.

Glaze Recipe:
1 cup confectioner's sugar OR blend evaporated cane juice until it is powder and add a little cornstarch)
2 tablespoons water (or lemon juice for lemon glaze)

Slowly add liquid (more or less than 2 tablespoons) until desired consistency is reached. The icing should be a little thick if cake is slightly warm when you put it on the cake.

Before my lifestyle change I would make a pound cake and my husband and I could eat it in a weekend. When my cousin Lisa introduced me to this recipe, it had been 12 loooooong years since I had tasted a pound cake. This one is soooooooo good. Whenever my cousin Camille is in town, we just have to make two cakes at a time. After all, we wouldn't want to waste the tofu!! We like to make a pina colada version….that's 1 tablespoon vanilla, $\frac{1}{2}$ tablespoon pineapple flavoring and $\frac{1}{2}$ tablespoon coconut flavoring - all alcohol-free of course!! Experiment and make yours like your family likes it!!! And, of course if you want to use all whole-wheat flour, please do. White wheat or whole wheat pastry would probably work best…plan to sift it though for a lighter final product!

Carob Brownies

1 cup whole wheat pastry flour

1 cup unbleached flour

$\frac{1}{2}$ cup sucanat

$\frac{1}{2}$ cup turbinado sugar

1 tablespoon EnerG egg replacer

1 heaping teaspoon Featherweight Baking Powder

1 teaspoon salt

$1\frac{1}{2}$ teaspoon Roma

$\frac{1}{2}$ cup carob (bean) powder

$\frac{3}{4}$ cup canola oil

1 cup plain soy milk

4 teaspoons alcohol-free vanilla flavoring

1 cup coarsely chopped walnuts and/or 1 cup carob chips (optional)

In a mixing bowl measure all dry ingredients. In another container, measure and mix all liquid ingredients. Pour liquid mixture into dry ingredients and mix together quickly. Add optional nuts and carob chips. Place batter into an 8x12 baking dish that has been sprayed with vegetable oil spray. Place in 350° oven and bake for 30-35 minutes or until toothpick inserted in center comes out clean. May frost if desired.

Serves 10-12

Carob Icing
2/3 cup soy margarine
$\frac{1}{2}$ cup carob powder
1 tablespoon Roma
1 teaspoon alcohol-free vanilla flavoring
3 cups organic powdered sugar
Soy milk to smooth

Cream margarine, carob powder and Roma. Add vanilla and powdered sugar (one cup at a time). Add soy milk to make a smooth, spreadable batter. Spread on cake.

Carob Rice Treats
4 cups your favorite carob chips
1 cup peanut butter
3-4 cups crispy brown rice cereal

Combine carob chips and peanut butter in a saucepan and heat on medium low until melted. When melted add brown rice cereal mixing well. Pack firmly into a vegetable sprayed baking dish. Refrigerate until mixture hardens. Cut into bars and serve. Store in refrigerator.

Yield: About 1 $\frac{1}{2}$ dozen bars

German Carob Cake

1 cup whole wheat pastry flour

1 $\frac{1}{2}$ cups all purpose, unbleached flour

$\frac{3}{4}$ cup toasted carob powder

1 cup Turbinado sugar

$\frac{1}{2}$ package MoriNu Vanilla Flavored Pudding Mix

2 tablespoons Roma

3 teaspoons Featherweight baking powder

2 EnerG Egg Replacers

$\frac{1}{2}$ teaspoon salt

$\frac{1}{2}$ cup canola oil

$\frac{1}{4}$ cup carob chips

$\frac{1}{2}$ cup pure maple syrup

1 teaspoon alcohol-free vanilla flavoring

1 cup soy milk

Hot water

Sift dry ingredients together in a mixing bowl. In another container melt carob chips. Add all other liquid ingredients to melted carob chips. Pour wet ingredients into dry and beat with an electric mixer until smooth. If necessary, add enough hot water to make a smooth batter. Pour into two round cake pans or one rectangular pan that has been sprayed with vegetable spray and floured. Bake at 350^0 until done—about 35-40 minutes. Cool slightly before turning out onto a rack to cool completely. Frost.

Serves 18-20

Coconut Pecan Frosting

1 cup pure maple syrup
½ cup water
1 teaspoon vanilla
2 tablespoons cornstarch
½ teaspoon salt
1 cup chopped coconut
1 cup chopped pecans

In a saucepan, heat maple syrup, water, vanilla, cornstarch and salt. Stir constantly until mixture starts to thicken. Remove from heat and add nuts and coconut. Cool to room temperature before using to frost top and center of cake. Double recipe to ice the entire cake.

Serves 18-20

Not Reese's Carob Candy*

1 cup your favorite carob chips
1 cup your favorite peanut butter
½-1 cup your favorite chopped nuts.

Place all ingredients in a microwave safe bowl. Microwave until chips are softened. Stir and pour batter into a lightly oiled pan. Chill. Cut into squares and serve. (You can also make in a double broiler).

Variations: Add mint
½-1 cup granola
Chopped coconut

Yield: about 1½ dozen pieces

Carob Coated Candy*

1 $\frac{1}{2}$ cups natural peanut butter
1 cup sucanat
$\frac{1}{2}$ cup honey
1 $\frac{1}{2}$ cups your favorite chopped nuts
1 $\frac{1}{2}$ cups your favorite ground granola
3 cups your favorite carob chips

In a large bowl, thoroughly mix all ingredients except carob chips. If mixture is too wet, add some more ground granola. Roll batter into balls or logs. Melt carob chips in a small bowl in the microwave or in a double boiler. Quickly dip ball/logs into melted carob and place on waxed paper lined cookie sheet. Let set until hard. Store in refrigerator.

Yield: about 1$\frac{1}{2}$ -2 dozen

Yummy Banana Nutty Bars (for kids only)*

4 bananas
3-4 cups your favorite carob chips
1-2 cups your favorite chopped nuts

In microwave or double boiler, melt carob chips. While carob chips are melting, peel and cut bananas in half. Place chopped nuts in small bowl. Remove melted carob chips from heat. Dip bananas into melted carob then in chopped nuts. Place on waxed paper to set. Keep refrigerated. Makes a great breakfast food for kids. (Frozen bananas make a great dessert).

Serves 4-6

Quick Peach Cobbler

½ cup Earth Balance margarine
1 cup your favorite soy, rice or nut milk
½ cup white whole wheat flour
½ cup unbleached, all-purpose flour
1 teaspoon Featherweight baking powder
Dash of salt
1 cup evaporated cane juice crystals
4 cups fresh, sliced peaches

Melt margarine in an 8x12 baking dish. In a bowl mix milk, flours, sugar baking powder and salt. Pour over melted margarine. Add sliced peaches but do not stir. Bake in a 375° oven until browning is noted. Serve with soy whipped cream.

Serves 8

My father-in-law didn't believe that you could make peach cobbler this way. He liked old school crust, and would stand in front of the oven when I made this one saying ooowhee! I don't believe it. Then he and my husband would clean the dish!!

Oatmeal Cookies

¾ cup Earth Balance Margarine

¾ cup Natural brown sugar

1/3 cup evaporated cane juice crystals

2 tablespoons EnerG egg replacer

½ cup soy milk

1 teaspoon vanilla

¾ cup whole wheat flour (pastry or white whole wheat)

¾ cup unbleached, all-purpose flour

2 teaspoon Featherweight baking powder, heaping

3 cups oats

1 teaspoon coriander

1 cup raisins (optional)

1 cup shredded coconut (optional)

Beat margarine and sugars until creamy. Add egg replacers, milk, and vanilla. Mix well. Add flour, baking powder, coriander and salt. Mix well. Stir in oats and optional ingredients. Drop by rounded tablespoonful onto ungreased cookie sheet. Bake 10-12 minutes or until golden brown in a 350° oven. Cool and serve

Yield: about 2 dozen cookies

Watermelon Pops

4-6 cups seeded watermelon chunks
1 can white grape raspberry juice, thawed

Blend watermelon and white grape raspberry juice until smooth. Add a little water if necessary for blending. Have children help you pour them into ice-pop molds. Freeze. Serve.

Variation: for Creamsicles add $\frac{3}{4}$ to 1 cup your favorite soy, nut or rice milk.

Island Fruit Punch

3 slices pineapple
1 cup pineapple juice
2 slices ripe mango
1 cup guava juice
$\frac{1}{2}$ cup orange juice
1 teaspoon lime juice
sweetener to taste
crushed ice

Place all ingredients into a blender. Fill with crushed ice and blend until smooth. Serve in tall glasses. Garnish with cherries/orange slices

Serves 4

Ivey's Hot Holiday Herb Tea
1 box NO Caffeine Peach Tea
1 quart water
3-4 lemons
Sucanat to taste

In a large pot, bring water to a boil. Add all tea bags to water and let steep about twenty minutes. Add enough water to make a gallon of tea. Squeeze juice of lemons into tea and. Add sucanat to taste. (Add more lemon juice for a more tart and delicious flavor and/or more water if it is too strong for your taste).

Variations: Add ½ gallon of apple juice or white grape/peach juice in place of ½ gallon water.
Serve on a buffet with cinnamon sticks and sliced lemons as garnish.

Yield: 1-1½ gallons

Party Punch 1
1-46 ounce can pineapple mango juice
1-64 ounce bottle white grape peach juice
1 -64 ounce bottle pulp-free orange juice
4-12 ounce bottles *The Switch* orange/tangerine flavor beverage

Mix all ingredients. Serve well chilled.

Yield: 20-25 servings

Hot Carob

1/3 cup turbinado sugar or sucanat
¼ cup carob powder
¼ cup Roma
Dash salt
1/3 cup water
1 quart your favorite soy or rice milk
¾ teaspoon alcohol-free vanilla

Place all ingredients in a blender and blend well. Pour into saucepan and heat slowly. Adjust to taste and serve.

Serves 4-6

Mocha Carob Banana Shake*

2 medium frozen bananas
1 ½ cups your favorite vanilla soy or rice milk
¾ cup your favorite carob chips
2 tablespoons pure maple syrup
1 tablespoon Roma

Blend all ingredients in blender until smooth. Serve.
Serves 2-4

Fruit Punch

1 – 64 oz. bottle apple juice
1 – 48 oz. bottle pineapple juice
1 – 64 oz. carton orange juice

Mix all ingredients. Chill thoroughly before serving. Serve in punch bowl garnished with orange slices.
Yield: 20-8 ounce servings

Party Punch 2

1 64-ounce carton of orange, peach, mango juice blend
1 46-ounce can of pineapple juice
1 32-ounce bottle mango juice
2 cups pink guava juice
2 cups water
6 peach flavored caffeine-free herbal tea bags
Optional: your favorite sweetener to taste

Mix all ingredients and let sit for at least two hours in order for tea to steep. Serve cold. Add carbonated water for a little zing!!

Cranberry Sparkle Punch

2 quarts cranberry juice cocktail, chilled
1 6-ounce can frozen pink lemonade concentrate, thawed
1 32-ounce bottle carbonated water, chilled

Mix cranberry juice cocktail and lemonade concentrate in punch bowl. Just before serving, stir in carbonated water.

Yield: 25 4-ounce servings

ONE DAY MEAL PLANNER

MEALS	FOOD ITEMS NEEDED	FOODS SERVED
		Whole Grain Bread, Cereal, Pasta, Rice ☐☐☐☐☐☐ __ __ __ __ __ **Vegetables** ☐☐☐ ___ ___ **Fruits** ☐☐ ___ ___ **Legume, Nut, Seed, Meat Alternatives** ☐☐ ___ **Non-Dairy Milk Products** ☐☐ ___ **Other** __ __ __ __

Recipes and Other Notes

ONE DAY MEAL PLANNER

MEALS	FOOD ITEMS NEEDED	FOODS SERVED
		Whole Grain Bread, Cereal, Pasta, Rice ☐☐☐☐☐☐ __ __ __ __ __ **Vegetables** ☐☐☐ ___ ___ **Fruits** ☐☐ ___ ___ **Legume, Nut, Seed, Meat Alternatives** ☐☐ ___ **Non-Dairy Milk Products** ☐☐ ___ **Other** ___ ___ ___ ___

Recipes and Other Notes

RECIPE MODIFICATION

Getting in the kitchen and experimenting is what makes food taste good to you. If you have some favorite recipes that need to be converted, try experimenting with new seasonings and ingredients, Keep record of what you do so that the new food will taste the same every time you do it.

RECIPE

OLD INGREDIENTS   NEW INGREDIENTS

_____   _____
_____   _____
_____   _____
_____   _____
_____   _____
_____   _____
_____   _____
_____   _____

METHOD

_____

_____

_____

_____

_____

_____

_____

DO AGAIN   NEVER DO AGAIN

RECIPE MODIFICATION

Getting in the kitchen and experimenting is what makes food taste good to you. If you have some favorite recipes that need to be converted, try experimenting with new seasonings and ingredients, Keep record of what you do so that the new food will taste the same every time you do it.

RECIPE

OLD INGREDIENTS

_____
_____
_____
_____
_____
_____
_____

NEW INGREDIENTS

_____
_____
_____
_____
_____
_____
_____

METHOD

_____
_____
_____
_____
_____
_____
_____

DO AGAIN   NEVER DO AGAIN

SHOPPING LIST

BREADS/CEREALS

FRUITS/VEGGIES

MEAT ALTERNATIVES

NON-DAIRY MILKS

OTHER

SHOPPING LIST

BREADS/CEREALS

FRUITS/VEGGIES

MEAT ALTERNATIVES

NON-DAIRY MILKS

OTHER

-NOTES-

RECIPE INDEX

BETTER BREAKFASTS

BREADS

SAUCES, SALADS, SPREADS AND SUCH

SOUPS AND STEWS

SWEET ENDINGS

If you liked the Cookin' Up Good Health Recipe Collection
You will love the Cookin' Up Good Health DVD's
Watch Donna prepare many of these recipes
right in the convenience of your own home or have a
group of your friends over and
cook up some good health together
To find out how to order log on to our website at
www.stillshoutin.com

Volume 1 – The Goodness of Grains
Phyt For Your Life

Volume 2 – Tofu What!?! and Goin 'Nuts!

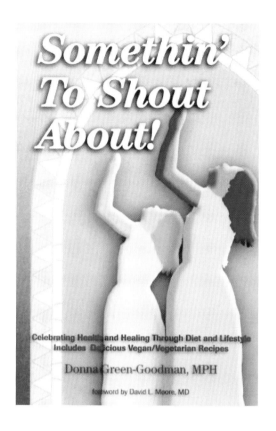

If you want to know how to completely change your lifestyle, and improve your health, you must get a copy of Donna's book Somethin' to Shout About!
She shares simple lifestyle principles that are simple, safe, scriptural and scientifically sound!
To get your copy visit our website at

www.stillshoutin.com

or go to

www.remnantpublications.com